Desserts for Dieters

LOW-CALORIE SWEET TREATS–ALL IRRESISTIBLE!

MARGARET HAPPEL

Butterick Publishing

The author and publisher thank the following for supplying props for use in the photography: La Cuisinière, 867 Madison Ave., New York, NY 10021; The Pottery Barn, 321 Tenth Ave., New York, NY 10011; and Villeroy and Boch, 41 Madison Ave., New York, NY 10010.

Book Design: *Betty Binns*

Photography: *Bill Helms*

Pictured on the front cover: Slim Pineapple Cheesecake (page 124).

Library of Congress Cataloging in Publication Data

Happel, Margaret.
  Desserts for dieters.

  Includes index.
  1. Low-calorie diet—Recipes. 2. Desserts.
I. Title.
RM222.2.H23   641.8′6   79-17718
ISBN 0-88421-066-9

CONTENTS

Introduction

If you're a dieter dreaming of desserts, you're in luck. Now you can enjoy your favorite part of the meal and still stick to that diet. DESSERTS FOR DIETERS shows how, through carefully developed low-calorie recipes.

Luscious cakes, cookies and pies, velvety custards and puddings, melt-in-your-mouth frozen confections, sweet and satisfying desserts of every description—they're all here. And they're all allowed. If you're skeptical, check the calorie count given for each dessert. In every case one serving is low enough in calories to comfortably fit into a weight-reducing diet of 1,200 calories per day.

Most of the recipes are sweetened with low quantities of sugar or honey or simply with the natural sweetness of the ingredients. Since many people must have noncaloric sweeteners for medical reasons, recipes using saccharin are also included. As this book goes to press, saccharin's pros and cons are still being debated, so using it is an individual choice. However, it is recommended that children and pregnant and nursing mothers avoid it. When in doubt, check with your doctor. If you don't need to use saccharin, one teaspoon of granulated sugar can be substituted for one tablespoon of saccharin wherever called for.

Whatever your pleasure—old-fashioned apple pie, rich chocolate pudding or a party-perfect baked Alaska—these desserts were created for you. Happy dieting!

Fruit Desserts

With their sun-ripened sweetness and beautiful appearance, fresh fruits are a dieter's best friend. Their natural sugar can satisfy that troublesome sweet tooth without piling on the calories. Many fruits are also high in vitamins A and C, and they add fiber to a diet. Best of all, they taste great.

Combined with key ingredients, like gelatin and spices and beaten egg whites, fruit can be transformed into the loveliest of low-cal desserts — Strawberry-Filled Meringues, for example, at only 51 calories a serving.

Here you'll find treats for every day, like Applesauce Cream, Frozen Banana Yogurt and Pineapple Parfait, which, by the way, registers a delightful 68 calories a serving. And there are company creations like Banana Pie in a graham cracker crust, Cherry Chiffon Pie and Raspberry-Apple Torte. The variety will help you stick to that diet. And, with the exception of Orange Cup Soufflés and Strawberry Dessert Omelet, these are all desserts that you can prepare in advance.

For perfect results, shop for the ripest, highest-quality seasonal fruits. When buying canned fruits, look for those packed in their own juice or in light rather than heavy syrup. Whole, frozen berries and unsweetened juices and applesauce are stocked by most supermarkets.

If you're looking for a bright, tasty ending for a meal, you've turned to the right chapter.

Ambrosia

2 medium-size yellow
  grapefruit
2 medium oranges
2 small dessert apples
½ cup orange juice
¼ cup shredded coconut

1. Peel grapefruit with sharp knife, cutting deeply enough to remove white pith. Cut grapefruit crosswise into ¼-inch slices. Peel oranges in the same way and cut into ¼-inch slices. Using apple corer or sharp knife, remove center core from apples. Cut crosswise into ¼-inch slices.

2. Arrange fruit slices in overlapping concentric circles in large shallow dessert bowl. Pour orange juice over all. Chill until serving time. Sprinkle with coconut.

Makes 4 servings. Each serving has 125 calories.

Triple Apple Dessert

1 envelope unflavored gelatin
1 tablespoon sugar
1 cup unsweetened apple
  juice
1 cup unsweetened
  applesauce
1 cup finely diced apple
¼ teaspoon almond extract
apple slices
mint sprigs

1. Sprinkle gelatin and sugar over ¼ cup of the apple juice in small saucepan; let stand for 5 minutes to soften. Place over very low heat just until gelatin is dissolved.

2. Stir in remaining ¾ cup apple juice, the applesauce, diced apple and almond extract. Pour into 3-cup mold. Chill until set, about 1 to 1½ hours.

3. Dip mold into hot water and invert onto serving platter; shake to release mold. Decorate with fresh unpeeled apple slices and mint sprigs.

Makes 4 servings. Each serving has 86 calories.

◎ *CalorieSaving Tip:* Use discretion in adding ingredients that impart a sweet flavor to a recipe, such as coconut or sugar. By using a little less, you can save 10 to 20 calories per serving. Never exceed the amount recommended in the recipe!

Applesauce Cream

2 cups unsweetened
applesauce
½ teaspoon cinnamon
¼ teaspoon nutmeg
1 cup evaporated skim milk,
chilled

1. Blend applesauce with cinnamon and nutmeg. Using electric mixer at high speed, beat evaporated milk in medium bowl until it is consistency of whipped topping.

2. Using rubber spatula, fold whipped milk into applesauce. Spoon into 4 parfait glasses; chill for 1 hour.

Makes 4 servings. Each serving has 86 calories.

Applesauce Parfaits

1 cup unsweetened
applesauce
1 cup lowfat, small curd
cottage cheese
1 cup fresh orange segments
¼ cup toasted shredded
coconut

1. In medium bowl, beat together applesauce and cottage cheese. Fold in orange segments.

2. Divide mixture among 4 parfait glasses. Chill until serving time. Sprinkle each with 1 tablespoon toasted coconut.

Makes 4 servings. Each serving has 103 calories.

Molded Apricot Fruit Dessert

1 envelope unflavored gelatin
2 cups apricot nectar
one 16-ounce can apricot
halves, drained
2 medium bananas, diced
1 cup seedless green grapes,
halved

1. Sprinkle gelatin over ½ cup of the apricot nectar in small saucepan; let stand for 5 minutes to soften. Place over very low heat just until gelatin is dissolved.

2. Stir in remaining apricot nectar, the drained apricots, diced banana and grape halves. Pour into 4-cup mold; chill until set, about 2 hours. Dip mold into hot water and invert onto serving platter; shake to release mold.

Makes 8 servings. Each serving has 127 calories.

Banana Pie

CRUST

1 tablespoon diet margarine

⅓ cup graham cracker crumbs

1 teaspoon sugar

FILLING

1 envelope unflavored gelatin

¼ cup water

2 eggs

2 cups skim milk

¼ cup sugar

2 medium bananas

1 teaspoon lemon juice

1 teaspoon vanilla extract

1. To make crust, grease 9-inch pie plate with diet margarine; mix graham cracker crumbs and teaspoon sugar and press onto bottom and sides of pie plate to coat. Chill.

2. To make filling, sprinkle gelatin over water in small custard cup; let stand for 5 minutes to soften. Meanwhile, beat together eggs and skim milk in top of double boiler; stir in ¼ cup sugar.

3. Place filling mixture over boiling water; cook, stirring constantly until sugar is dissolved and mixture thickens and lightly coats back of wooden spoon. Stir in softened gelatin to dissolve.

4. In large bowl, crush bananas with fork, adding lemon juice to prevent discoloration. Add vanilla extract. Stir in gelatin-milk mixture. Chill until semi-set, 30 to 45 minutes.

5. Using electric mixer at high speed, beat filling until light and fluffy. Spoon into prepared pie plate. Chill until completely set, 1½ to 2 hours.

Makes 8 servings. Each serving has 112 calories.

Frozen Banana Yogurt

2 medium bananas

2 tablespoons lemon juice

1 tablespoon sugar

⅛ teaspoon salt

1 cup lowfat unflavored yogurt

1. In medium bowl, thoroughly mash banana with fork, blending in lemon juice. Stir in sugar and salt.

2. Stir in yogurt, mixing well. Pour into ice cube tray (divider removed). Freeze until almost set, about 1 hour. Place in medium bowl; using electric mixer at high speed, beat until creamy.

3. Return yogurt mixture to ice cube tray; freeze until very firm, about 2 hours. Place ⅓ cup frozen yogurt in each of 4 parfait glasses. Serve immediately.

Makes 4 servings. Each serving has 91 calories.

Blueberry Parfaits

1 envelope unflavored gelatin
1¾ cups skim milk
¼ cup sugar
2 teaspoons rum extract or vanilla extract
3 egg whites
2 cups fresh or frozen blueberries, thawed

1. Sprinkle gelatin over ¼ cup of the skim milk in small custard cup; let stand for 5 minutes to soften. Meanwhile, heat remaining 1½ cups skim milk and the sugar in medium saucepan over low heat; stir to dissolve sugar.

2. Stir in softened gelatin to dissolve. Cool slightly; stir in rum or vanilla extract, then pour into large bowl. Chill until semi-set, at least 1 hour.

3. Using electric mixer at high speed, beat egg whites in medium bowl until stiff. Using mixer at high speed, beat gelatin mixture until light and fluffy. Using rubber spatula, fold egg whites into gelatin mixture.

4. Layer one-fourth of the gelatin mixture alternately with ½ cup blueberries in each of 4 parfait glasses. Chill until served.

Makes 4 servings. Each serving has 143 calories.

Cherry Chiffon Pie

1 envelope unflavored gelatin
¾ cup water
3 eggs, separated
3 tablespoons sugar
1 teaspoon almond extract
one 16-ounce can water-packed cherries, drained and finely chopped
2 to 3 drops red food coloring

1. Sprinkle gelatin over ¼ cup of the water in small custard cup; let stand for 5 minutes to soften. Meanwhile, blend egg yolks, 2 tablespoons of the sugar and the remaining ½ cup water in small saucepan.

2. Heat over low heat, stirring constantly, until mixture thickens and lightly coats back of wooden spoon. Stir in softened gelatin to dissolve. Cool mixture; stir in almond extract and chill until syrupy. Stir in cherries and food coloring.

3. Using electric mixer at high speed, beat egg whites in medium bowl until stiff. Using rubber spatula, fold into cherry mixture. Spoon into 9-inch pie plate. Chill until completely set, 1½ to 2 hours.

Makes 8 servings. Each serving has 76 calories.

Cranberry-Orange Cream

1 envelope unflavored gelatin

1¾ cups cranberry juice cocktail

½ teaspoon grated orange rind

½ cup lowfat, small curd cottage cheese

3 medium oranges, peeled and cut into segments

1. Sprinkle gelatin over ½ cup of the cranberry juice in small saucepan; let stand for 5 minutes to soften. Place over very low heat just until gelatin is dissolved.

2. Stir in remaining cranberry juice and the orange rind. Pour half of cranberry juice mixture into blender container; add cottage cheese. Blend at high speed for 15 seconds or until mixture is smooth.

3. Place pureed mixture and remaining cranberry juice mixture in medium bowl; chill until semi-set, about 1 hour. Fold in orange segments. Divide among 4 dessert dishes; chill until completely set, 1½ to 2 hours.

Makes 4 servings. Each serving has 141 calories.

Cranberry Shimmer

1 envelope unflavored gelatin

1¾ cups cranberry juice cocktail

1 cup unsweetened applesauce

½ cup crushed pineapple in natural juices

½ teaspoon grated lemon rind

1. Sprinkle gelatin over ½ cup of the cranberry juice in small saucepan; let stand for 5 minutes to soften. Place over very low heat just until gelatin is dissolved.

2. Stir in remaining cranberry juice, the applesauce, un-drained pineapple and lemon rind. Place in 3-cup mold. Chill until set, about 1½ hours. Dip mold into hot water and invert onto serving platter; shake to release mold.

Makes 4 servings. Each serving has 113 calories.

Note: Mold can be chilled until semi-set. Divide among 4 dessert dishes; chill to set completely.

Fruit Cocktail Pie

one 10-ounce package
  piecrust mix

one 20-ounce can pineapple
  chunks in natural juices

one 10-ounce package frozen
  strawberries, thawed

1 medium banana, sliced

1 tablespoon cornstarch

1 teaspoon grated lemon rind

1. Prepare piecrust mix according to label directions. Divide in half; wrap and refrigerate one portion for another use. Roll out remaining half to line 8-inch pie plate. Trim and flute edge of pastry. Prick pie shell well; chill or freeze for 15 minutes. Bake according to label directions for empty pie shell; set on wire rack to cool completely.

2. Drain and reserve juice from pineapple and strawberries. In medium bowl, combine pineapple and strawberries with sliced banana; set aside.

3. In medium saucepan, blend cornstarch and lemon rind with reserved fruit juices; bring to boiling point over medium heat, stirring constantly until mixture thickens.

4. Pour thickened liquid over fruit mixture; stir gently to combine. Cool slightly before pouring into pastry shell. Chill until completely set, about 1½ hours.

Makes 8 servings. Each serving has 165 calories.

Fruit and Custard

1 cup sliced fresh strawberries

1 cup fresh or frozen
  blueberries

1 cup skim milk

1 egg

2 tablespoons sugar

¼ teaspoon nutmeg

1. Place ¼ cup each strawberries and blueberries in each of 4 dessert dishes; chill.

2. In small saucepan, heat together skim milk, egg, sugar and nutmeg. Cook over low heat, stirring constantly until mixture thickens and lightly coats back of wooden spoon.

3. Chill custard for at least 1 hour; spoon over chilled fruit.

Makes 4 servings. Each serving has 101 calories.

Fruit Floating Island

2 egg whites
⅛ teaspoon cream of tartar
⅛ teaspoon salt
2 tablespoons sugar
1 cup fresh whole strawberries, hulled
one 20-ounce can pineapple chunks in natural juices

1. Using electric mixer at high speed, beat egg whites, cream of tartar and salt in medium bowl, until soft peaks form. Sprinkle in 1 tablespoon of the sugar; beat until egg whites are stiff.

2. Fill 12-inch skillet half full with water; add remaining 1 tablespoon sugar. Bring to boiling point over medium heat; reduce heat to low.

3. Drop meringue by rounded tablespoonfuls, four at a time, into simmering water. Poach gently for about 4 minutes, carefully turning once with slotted spoon. Using slotted spoon, carefully lift meringues from water; place on clean towel.

4. In electric blender, puree strawberries and undrained pineapple at high speed for 5 seconds. Pour into 4 individual dessert dishes; top with meringues and chill until serving time.

Makes 4 servings. Each serving has 138 calories.

Citrus-Grape Mold

1 envelope unflavored gelatin
¼ cup sugar
¾ cup orange juice
¼ cup lemon juice
2 teaspoons grated lemon rind
1 teaspoon grated orange rind
½ teaspoon almond extract
4 egg whites
1 cup seedless green grapes, halved

1. In medium saucepan, combine gelatin, sugar, orange juice, lemon juice, lemon rind and orange rind. Heat over very low heat just until gelatin is dissolved.

2. Pour into large bowl; stir in almond extract. Cool, and chill until semi-set, about 30 to 45 minutes.

3. Using electric mixer at high speed, beat egg whites in large bowl until stiff. Using mixer at high speed, beat gelatin mixture until light and fluffy.

4. Using rubber spatula, fold egg whites into gelatin mixture. Spoon into 1½-quart mold, sprinkling grape halves throughout mixture. Chill until set, at least 2 hours. Dip mold into hot water and invert onto serving platter; shake to release mold.

Makes 4 servings. Each serving has 118 calories.

Mandarin Mold

1 envelope unflavored gelatin
¾ cup orange juice
1½ cups buttermilk
2 tablespoons honey
1 teaspoon grated lemon rind
one 11-ounce can mandarin
   oranges, drained

1. Sprinkle gelatin over ¼ cup of the orange juice in small saucepan; let stand for 5 minutes to soften. Place over very low heat just until gelatin is dissolved.

2. Stir in remaining ½ cup orange juice, the buttermilk, honey and lemon rind. Arrange orange segments in spiral pattern over bottom of 3-cup mold and pour in ½ cup of the gelatin mixture; chill until slightly set, about 15 minutes.

3. Pour in remaining buttermilk-gelatin mixture; chill until completely set, about 1½ hours. Dip mold into hot water and invert onto serving platter; shake to release mold.

Makes 4 servings. Each serving has 137 calories.

Melon and Blueberry Mold

2 envelopes unflavored gelatin
2 tablespoons sugar
½ cup cold water
2 cups orange juice
2 tablespoons lemon juice
1 cup fresh honeydew melon
   balls
1 cup fresh or frozen
   blueberries

1. Sprinkle gelatin and sugar over cold water in medium saucepan; let stand for 5 minutes to soften. Place over very low heat just until gelatin is dissolved.

2. Stir in orange juice and lemon juice. Chill until semi-set, about 30 minutes. Stir in melon balls and blueberries.

3. Pour into 4-cup mold; chill until completely set, about 1 hour. Dip mold into hot water and invert onto serving platter; shake to release mold.

Makes 4 servings. Each serving has 128 calories.

Molded Summer Dessert

1 envelope unflavored gelatin
¼ cup sugar
1¼ cups water
¼ cup lemon juice
1 teaspoon grated lemon rind
½ cup sliced strawberries
½ cup fresh or frozen
  blueberries
1 small banana, sliced
½ cup seedless green grapes,
  halved

1. Combine gelatin, sugar and ½ cup of the water in small saucepan; let stand for 5 minutes to soften. Place over very low heat just until gelatin is dissolved.

2. Stir in remaining ¾ cup water, the lemon juice and lemon rind. Chill until syrupy, about 15 minutes.

3. Fold in strawberries, blueberries, banana and grape halves. Pour into 1-quart mold; chill until completely set, at least 1 hour. Dip mold into hot water and invert onto serving platter; shake to release mold.

Makes 4 servings. Each serving has 108 calories.

Orange Cup Soufflés

4 large oranges
1 tablespoon sugar
1 tablespoon flour
¼ cup skim milk
2 eggs, separated
¼ cup shredded coconut
¼ cup chopped pecans or
  walnuts
4 teaspoons orange
  marmalade

1. Preheat oven to 375° F.

2. Cut ½-inch slice from tops of oranges; using teaspoon, scoop out pulp, being careful not to pierce skin. Set orange shells aside. Press some of pulp through strainer to yield 1 tablespoon orange juice; reserve juice. Chop remaining pulp to measure ¼ cup; set aside.

3. In small saucepan, combine sugar, flour and skim milk, stirring to keep smooth; stir in reserved orange juice. Bring mixture to boiling point over low heat, stirring constantly. Remove from heat; stir in egg yolks and coconut.

4. Using electric mixer at high speed, beat egg whites in medium bowl until stiff. Fold into yolk-coconut mixture.

5. Place 1 tablespoon reserved pulp and 1 teaspoon marmalade in bottom of each orange shell. Fill each shell with soufflé mixture. Bake for 15 to 20 minutes, until puffed and browned.

Makes 4 servings. Each serving has 158 calories.

Yogurt Cream à l'Orange

2½ cups orange juice
¼ cup quick-cooking tapioca
one 8-ounce container lowfat orange-flavored yogurt
¼ cup shredded coconut

1. In medium saucepan, combine orange juice and tapioca; bring to boiling point over low heat, stirring constantly.

2. Remove from heat; cool completely and chill for 30 minutes. Stir in yogurt and coconut. Divide among 4 dessert dishes; chill.

Makes 4 servings. Each serving has 145 calories.

Peach Meringue Tart

2 egg whites
½ teaspoon cream of tartar
2 tablespoons sugar
½ teaspoon vanilla extract
¼ teaspoon almond extract
4 medium-size fresh peaches, sliced
⅓ cup nonfat dry milk powder
⅓ cup ice water

1. Preheat oven to 275° F.

2. Using electric mixer at high speed, beat egg whites and cream of tartar in medium bowl, until soft peaks form. Sprinkle in sugar, 1 tablespoon at a time; beat after each addition until egg whites are stiff.

3. Fold in vanilla and almond extracts. Spread meringue in an 8-inch pie plate to form a shell. Bake for 1 hour. Set on wire rack to cool completely.

4. Place sliced peaches in cooled shell. Using electric mixer at high speed, beat dry milk powder and ice water in medium bowl until mixture is consistency of whipped topping. Swirl over top of peaches. Serve immediately.

Makes 6 servings. Each serving has 81 calories.

Pear-Pineapple Foams

1 envelope unflavored gelatin
¾ cup orange juice
one 8-ounce container lowfat
  pineapple-flavored yogurt
1 medium-size ripe pear
2 egg whites

1. Sprinkle gelatin over orange juice in small saucepan; let stand for 5 minutes to soften. Place over very low heat just until gelatin is dissolved.

2. Pour mixture into medium bowl; stir in yogurt. Chill until mixture reaches consistency of unbeaten egg whites, about 20 minutes.

3. Pare and core pear; chop finely. Using electric mixer at high speed, beat egg whites in medium bowl until stiff. Using rubber spatula, fold egg whites and chopped pear into gelatin mixture. Divide among 4 glass dessert dishes.

Makes 4 servings. Each serving has 95 calories.

Lemony Pineapple Mold

2 envelopes unflavored gelatin
½ cup cold water
¾ cup boiling water
one 6-ounce can frozen
  lemonade concentrate
one 16-ounce can pineapple
  chunks in natural juices
1 tablespoon lemon or lime
  juice

1. Sprinkle gelatin over cold water in medium bowl; let stand for 5 minutes to soften. Add boiling water; stir until gelatin is completely dissolved.

2. Stir in frozen lemonade concentrate, undrained pineapple chunks and lemon or lime juice. Pour into 4-cup mold; chill until completely set, about 2 hours. Dip mold into hot water and invert onto serving platter; shake to release mold.

Makes 4 servings. Each serving has 68 calories.

Peppermint-Pineapple Cream

1 envelope unflavored gelatin
2 cups skim milk
¼ cup sugar
¼ teaspoon peppermint extract
2 to 3 drops green food coloring
one 8-ounce can pineapple tidbits in natural juices

1. Sprinkle gelatin over ¼ cup of the skim milk in small custard cup; let stand for 5 minutes to soften. Heat remaining 1¾ cups skim milk to boiling point in small saucepan over medium heat. Stir in softened gelatin to dissolve.

2. Cool slightly; stir in peppermint extract and food coloring. Pour into 9 x 5 x 3-inch loaf pan; chill to set completely, 1½ to 2 hours.

3. To serve, cut gelatin into 4 portions and top each serving with ¼ cup undrained pineapple tidbits.

Makes 4 servings. Each serving has 147 calories.

Pineapple-Cheese Loaf

one 8-ounce can crushed pineapple in natural juices
1 envelope unflavored gelatin
one 16-ounce container lowfat, small curd cottage cheese
1 egg
¼ cup sugar
1 teaspoon vanilla extract
½ teaspoon grated lemon rind
mint sprigs

1. Drain juice from pineapple into small saucepan; reserve pineapple. Sprinkle gelatin over juice; let stand for 5 minutes to soften. Place over very low heat just until gelatin is dissolved.

2. Meanwhile, use electric mixer to beat together cottage cheese, egg, sugar, vanilla extract, lemon rind and reserved pineapple in medium bowl. Stir in dissolved gelatin.

3. Pour mixture into 9 x 5 x 3-inch loaf pan. Chill for at least 2 hours. Unmold onto serving platter and garnish with mint sprigs.

Makes 8 servings. Each serving has 97 calories.

Pineapple Mousse

1 envelope unflavored gelatin
1 tablespoon sugar
½ cup water
1 cup evaporated skim milk
½ teaspoon rum extract
one 8-ounce can crushed pineapple in natural juices, drained
¼ cup flaked coconut

1. In small saucepan, blend sugar and gelatin. Stir in water; heat over very low heat, stirring constantly, until gelatin is dissolved. Pour into medium bowl. Stir in evaporated milk and rum extract. Chill until semi-set, 30 to 45 minutes.

2. Using electric mixer at high speed, beat mixture until light and fluffy; fold in drained pineapple and coconut.

3. Divide mixture among four 6-ounce custard cups or individual soufflé dishes. Chill until completely set, about 1 hour.

Makes 4 servings. Each serving has 122 calories.

Pineapple Parfait

one 8-ounce can crushed pineapple in natural juices, drained
1 cup lowfat, small curd cottage cheese
½ cup evaporated skim milk, chilled
¼ teaspoon rum extract
1 cup sliced fresh strawberries

1. In small bowl, blend together drained pineapple and cottage cheese.

2. Using electric mixer at high speed, beat evaporated milk in another small bowl until it is consistency of whipped topping. Fold into pineapple mixture along with rum extract.

3. Layer 2 tablespoons pineapple mixture and 2 tablespoons berries in each of 4 large parfait glasses. Repeat layering; top each portion with ¼ cup pineapple mixture.

Makes 4 servings. Each serving has 88 calories.

⊗ *CalorieSaving Tip:* Read labels to cut calories. If you're really paring down your calorie count, read every label when you shop. The caloric content of packaged products can vary considerably from brand to brand. Comparison shop to find the item with the lowest number of calories.

Raisin-Grapenut Pudding

1½ cups water
½ cup grapenuts
¼ cup quick-cooking tapioca
¼ cup brown sugar, lightly packed
¼ cup chopped golden raisins
½ teaspoon vanilla extract
⅓ cup nonfat dry milk powder
⅓ cup ice water

1. In top of double boiler, combine water, grapenuts, tapioca, brown sugar, golden raisins and vanilla extract.

2. Cook over boiling water until mixture thickens, about 10 minutes, stirring constantly. Spoon into four 6-ounce custard cups or individual dessert dishes.

3. Using electric mixer at high speed, beat dry milk powder and ice water in small bowl until mixture is consistency of whipped topping. Serve with warm pudding.

Makes 4 servings. Each serving has 159 calories.

Rasberry-Apple Torte

¼ cup diet margarine
2 cups graham cracker crumbs
2 cups unsweetened applesauce
two 10-ounce packages frozen raspberries, thawed and drained

1. Melt diet margarine in large skillet over medium heat; stir in graham cracker crumbs. Heat, stirring constantly, until crumbs are crisp; cool completely.

2. Spread ½ cup of the crumbs in bottom of 8-inch springform pan, patting to make firm layer. Top with 1 cup of the applesauce; sprinkle with ½ cup graham cracker crumbs.

3. In electric blender, puree raspberries at high speed, until smooth, about 10 seconds. Spread half over dessert; top with ½ cup graham cracker crumbs; spread remaining raspberries over crumbs.

4. Sprinkle with ½ cup graham cracker crumbs; spread remaining 1 cup applesauce over crumbs. Sprinkle with remaining crumbs. Chill torte for 24 hours before serving.

Makes 12 servings. Each serving has 126 calories.

Strawberry Cream Pie

one 10-ounce package
  piecrust mix

1 envelope unflavored gelatin

½ cup water

one 10-ounce package frozen
  strawberries, thawed and
  drained

¾ cup ice water

½ cup nonfat dry milk powder

1. Prepare piecrust mix according to label directions. Divide in half; wrap and refrigerate one portion for another use. Roll out remaining half to line 8-inch pie plate. Trim and flute edge of pastry. Prick pie shell well; chill or freeze for 15 minutes. Bake according to label directions for empty pie shell; set on wire rack to cool completely.

2. Sprinkle gelatin over water in small saucepan; let stand for 5 minutes to soften. Place over low heat just until gelatin is dissolved.

3. In small bowl, combine gelatin, drained strawberries and ¼ cup of the ice water; chill until thickened, about 15 to 20 minutes.

4. Sprinkle dry milk powder over remaining ½ cup ice water in large bowl. Using electric mixer at high speed, beat until stiff peaks form.

5. Using mixer at high speed, beat gelatin-strawberry mixture until light and foamy. Using rubber spatula, gently fold into dry milk mixture; spoon into pie shell and chill until completely set, about 1½ hours.

Makes 8 servings. Each serving has 119 calories.

○ *CalorieSaving Tip:* Whether it's canned or frozen, always try to buy unsweetened fruit. To thaw unsweetened frozen fruit, place it in a microwave oven for 1 minute (on the "defrost" setting if your oven has one), or put the unopened package in a bowl of warm water for 20 to 30 minutes, changing the water if necessary to maintain the warm temperature.

Strawberry Dessert Omelet

6 eggs
¼ cup water
¼ teaspoon salt
1 tablespoon diet margarine
1 cup fresh strawberries, crushed
1 tablespoon confectioners' sugar

1. In large bowl, beat together eggs, water and salt. Melt diet margarine in large skillet with nonstick finish over medium heat. Add egg mixture; cook, stirring constantly, until thickened, shiny and moist.

2. Let eggs cook for 1 minute without stirring to lightly brown undersurface. Place crushed strawberries in a band across the third of omelet nearest handle of skillet.

3. Using large spatula, roll omelet toward far edge of skillet, enclosing filling. Tilt onto warm serving platter. Sprinkle with confectioners' sugar. Serve immediately.

Makes 4 servings. Each serving has 151 calories.

Strawberry-Filled Meringues

4 egg whites, at room temperature
¼ teaspoon cream of tartar
2 tablespoons sugar
2 cups fresh strawberries
¼ cup unsweetened grapefruit juice

1. Preheat oven to 250° F. Line cookie sheet with brown paper.

2. Using electric mixer at high speed, beat egg whites and cream of tartar in large bowl, until foamy. Add sugar, 1 tablespoon at a time; beat after each addition until soft peaks form.

3. Fill pastry bag with mixture and press meringues onto paper-lined cookie sheet in round or oval shells 3 to 4 inches in diameter and 1 inch high; form a solid base first, then build up sides. Or shape shells by mounding meringue into 6 piles on paper-lined cookie sheet and, using back of wet teaspoon, make a hollow in center of each.

4. Bake for 1½ hours; cool completely. Using sharp-edged spatula, carefully remove meringues to wire rack.

5. Meanwhile, hull, wash and slice strawberries; place in bowl and toss with grapefruit juice. Chill. To serve, fill meringues with strawberries.

Makes 6 servings. Each serving has 51 calories.

Strawberry Sponge

½ cup evaporated skim milk
2 eggs, separated
½ teaspoon vanilla extract
one 10-ounce package frozen
  strawberries, thawed

1. Heat evaporated milk and egg yolks in top of double boiler over boiling water; stir for about 5 minutes, until mixture thickens and lightly coats back of wooden spoon. Remove from heat; add vanilla extract. Cool completely.

2. In electric blender, puree strawberries until smooth, about 15 seconds. Stir into cooled custard.

3. Using electric mixer at high speed, beat egg whites in medium bowl until stiff peaks form. Fold into custard mixture. Pour into 4 dessert dishes.

Makes 4 servings. Each serving has 168 calories.

Strawberry-Yogurt Pie

4 egg whites
¼ teaspoon cream of tartar
¼ teaspoon salt
¼ cup sugar
½ teaspoon vanilla extract
2 cups fresh strawberries
1 cup lowfat unflavored yogurt

1. Preheat oven to 250° F.

2. Using electric mixer at high speed, beat egg whites, cream of tartar and salt in large bowl until soft peaks form. Add sugar, 1 tablespoon at a time; beat after each addition until stiff peaks form. With mixer at low speed, stir in vanilla extract.

3. Spread meringue in 8-inch pie plate to form a shell. Bake for 1 to 1½ hours or until firm and light brown. Set on wire rack to cool completely.

4. Hull, wash and dry strawberries; slice thickly. Fold into yogurt and chill until serving time.

5. To serve, spoon strawberry-yogurt mixture into meringue shell. Serve immediately; this dessert does not keep well.

Makes 8 servings. Each serving has 59 calories.

Summer Fruit Bowl with Yogurt

1 cup fresh strawberries, sliced

½ cup diced cantaloupe

½ cup fresh or frozen
   blueberries

1 cup diced pear

½ cup orange juice

½ cup lowfat unflavored
   yogurt

1. Combine strawberries, cantaloupe, blueberries, pear and orange juice in large serving bowl. Toss to mix well; chill until serving time.

2. To serve, divide fruit among 4 individual dessert dishes; top each serving with 2 tablespoons yogurt.

Makes 4 servings. Each serving has 75 calories. Shown on page 65.

Three-Fruit Cream

1 envelope unflavored gelatin

1 cup orange juice

½ cup lowfat sour cream

1 tablespoon sugar

½ cup canned pitted water-
   pack cherries

1 medium banana, thinly
   sliced

1. Sprinkle gelatin over ½ cup of the orange juice in small saucepan; let stand for 5 minutes to soften. Place over very low heat just until gelatin is dissolved.

2. Stir in remaining ½ cup orange juice, the sour cream and sugar. Chill until semi-set, about 1 hour.

3. Fold in cherries and banana; divide among 4 parfait glasses and chill until completely set, about 1½ to 2 hours.

Makes 4 servings. Each serving has 140 calories.

Baked Desserts

Fruit and spice and everything nice go into these luscious dishes, which are sweetened with only small amounts of sugar. Especially nice in winter are the warm fruit crunches and creamy custards. Or perhaps you prefer pies or soufflés. They're all here. With a couple of exceptions, including the Nut Soufflés, most of the recipes in this chapter contain between 100 and 150 calories per serving — hard to beat.

Many of these desserts are flavored with sweet spices that please the palate without adding a pound. Baked Pear Halves, sweetened with honey and cinnamon, have only 87 calories a serving, and a classic Vanilla Soufflé, only 90. And when you serve the creamy Coconut Custard Pie from this chapter, you'll probably have trouble convincing your friends it has only 101 calories a slice.

To keep calorie counts at a minimum, be sure to use the low-cal ingredients called for in the recipes. And cook desserts until they are just done. Overcooked desserts shrink and dry out so that each serving is smaller, though the calorie count remains the same. A skimpy first serving is a woeful temptation to the reluctant dieter contemplating seconds.

Do you hanker for something sweet and comfortingly warm? Any one of the following recipes will fill the bill.

Apple Crunch

5 large apples, peeled, cored
  and sliced
½ cup unsweetened apple
  juice
1 cup cornflakes
2 tablespoons brown sugar
1 teaspoon cinnamon
¼ teaspoon nutmeg
¼ cup diet margarine, melted

1. Preheat oven to 350° F.

2. Arrange apple slices in 8-inch pie plate; pour in apple juice.

3. In medium bowl, mix together cornflakes, brown sugar, cinnamon and nutmeg. Stir in melted diet margarine with fork.

4. Spread cornflake mixture over apples; bake for 30 minutes, until apples are tender and crust is crisp.

Makes 8 servings. Each serving has 104 calories.

Peachy Cranberry Crunch

½ cup quick-cooking oatmeal
¼ cup flour
2 tablespoons brown sugar
¼ cup diet margarine, melted
1 cup fresh cranberries
one 8-ounce can sliced
  peaches, drained

1. Preheat oven to 375° F.

2. In small bowl, mix together oatmeal, flour and brown sugar. Stir in melted diet margarine with fork; set aside.

3. Using food processor, blender or coarse setting of meat grinder, coarsely chop cranberries. Mix cranberries with drained peach slices.

4. Divide fruit mixture among 4 lightly greased 6-ounce custard cups. Spread one-fourth of oatmeal topping over each. Bake for 25 to 30 minutes, until cranberries are tender and topping is crisp.

Makes 4 servings. Each serving has 148 calories.

CalorieSaving Tip: Tablespoon for tablespoon, honey contains more calories than sugar, but you need less honey to sweeten a dessert to the same intensity. There is no type of sugar that is "better" for you—all crystal-type sugars, no matter what their color, have the same calorie count, so use them sparingly. Brown sugars are more flavorful, though, because of their molasses content.

Marinated Hot Fruit Compote

2 large pears
2 large apples
1 cup whole strawberries
1 cup fresh or frozen
   blueberries

   MARINADE

⅔ cup orange juice
2 tablespoons lemon juice
2 tablespoons honey
3 whole cloves
¼ teaspoon cinnamon

1. Preheat oven to 350° F.

2. Pare and core pears; cut each into 6 wedges. Prepare apples the same way. Hull and wash strawberries; wash fresh blueberries. Place all fruit in 1½-quart casserole; toss to mix.

3. To make marinade, combine orange juice, lemon juice, honey, cloves and cinnamon in small saucepan. Heat to dissolve honey. Pour marinade over fruit. Cover casserole and bake for 15 to 20 minutes, until piping hot.

Makes 8 servings. Each serving has 106 calories.

Baked Pear Halves

2 large ripe pears
lemon juice
½ cup water
1 tablespoon honey
¼ cup graham cracker
   crumbs
1 tablespoon diet margarine,
   melted
¼ teaspoon cinnamon

1. Preheat oven to 425° F.

2. Pare pears and cut lengthwise in half; using teaspoon, scoop out core. Rub a little lemon juice over all cut surfaces to prevent discoloration.

3. Place pears core side up in lightly greased 8 x 8 x 2-inch baking dish; add water to dish. Drizzle a little honey over each pear half. Cover dish tightly with foil.

4. Bake pears for 15 to 20 minutes or until tender. Remove foil. Mix together graham cracker crumbs, melted diet margarine and cinnamon; sprinkle over pears. Bake an additional 10 minutes.

Makes 4 servings. Each serving has 87 calories.

Maple Pears

4 medium pears
2 tablespoons lemon juice
⅓ cup maple syrup
¼ cup water
1½ teaspoons grated lemon rind
2 tablespoons diet margarine

1. Preheat oven to 350° F.

2. Pare pears and cut lengthwise in half; using teaspoon, scoop out core. Brush pears with lemon juice to prevent discoloration. Place pears cut side down in 9-inch pie plate.

3. Heat maple syrup, water and lemon rind to simmering point in small saucepan. Pour mixture over pears; dot pears with diet margarine.

4. Bake for 40 to 45 minutes or until pears are tender, basting every 10 minutes with syrup mixture and turning cut side up halfway through cooking period.

Makes 4 servings. Each serving has 193 calories.

Baked Orangy Pears

4 large pears
½ cup finely chopped orange segments
¼ cup finely chopped golden raisins
1 teaspoon grated lemon rind
½ teaspoon cinnamon
2 cups orange juice

1. Preheat oven to 350° F.

2. Remove core from each pear with apple corer; set pears in four 10-ounce custard cups. Combine chopped oranges, golden raisins, lemon rind and cinnamon in small bowl; stuff center of each pear with one-fourth mixture. Pour ½ cup orange juice around each.

3. Set custard cups on large baking sheet. Bake for 20 to 30 minutes, until pears are tender, basting frequently with orange juice. Cool slightly before serving.

Makes 4 servings. Each serving has 209 calories.

Pineapple Crumble

one 16-ounce can pineapple
  tidbits in natural juices,
  drained
¾ cup graham cracker
  crumbs
1 tablespoon brown sugar
1 tablespoon diet margarine,
  melted
¼ teaspoon cinnamon

1. Preheat oven to 350° F.

2. Place drained pineapple tidbits in 8 x 8 x 2-inch baking dish. In small bowl, combine graham cracker crumbs, brown sugar, melted diet margarine and cinnamon; toss to mix well.

3. Sprinkle crumb mixture over pineapple. Bake for 15 to 20 minutes or until pineapple is hot and topping is crisp.

Makes 4 servings. Each serving has 122 calories.

Note: Instead of baking, broil this dessert 8 inches from heat for 5 minutes if desired.

Blueberry Meringue Torte

½ cup sifted cake flour
¾ teaspoon baking powder
3 eggs
½ cup granulated sugar
1 teaspoon grated lemon rind

  TOPPING

1 cup fresh or frozen
  blueberries
¼ cup water
1 tablespoon honey
2 egg whites
2 tablespoons confectioners'
  sugar

1. Preheat oven to 375° F. Sift together sifted cake flour and baking powder; set aside.

2. Using electric mixer at high speed, beat eggs in large bowl until thick and lemon colored. Gradually add granulated sugar, 2 tablespoons at a time; beat well after each addition.

3. Beat in lemon rind. With electric mixer at low speed, blend in flour mixture, one third at a time, making sure flour is absorbed after each addition.

4. Spoon batter into 8 x 8 x 2-inch baking pan with nonstick finish; bake for 20 minutes or until cake tester inserted in center comes out clean. Set pan on wire rack to cool for 10 minutes; remove shell from pan and place on wire rack to cool completely.

5. To make topping, combine blueberries, water and honey in small saucepan. Simmer, covered, over low heat until blueberries are tender and skins burst, about 10 minutes; cool.

6. Using electric mixer at high speed, beat egg whites in medium bowl until soft peaks form; gradually add confectioners' sugar, beating until egg whites are stiff.

7. To serve, cut cake into 2-inch squares; place 1 square on each of 4 dessert plates. Frost with meringue and top with blueberry sauce. Wrap and freeze remaining cake for later use.

Makes 4 servings. Each serving has 109 calories.

Grapefruit-Orange Alaska

2 medium grapefruit
2 medium oranges
3 egg whites
⅛ teaspoon cream of tartar
⅛ teaspoon salt
2 tablespoons sugar

1. Preheat oven to 350° F.

2. Using sharp knife, cut grapefruit in half; cut to free sections and remove fibrous center. Place sections in medium bowl.

3. Peel oranges, cutting deeply enough to remove white pith. Cut between fruit and membrane to loosen sections. Remove seeds; combine orange sections with grapefruit sections, tossing to mix well.

4. Using electric mixer at high speed, beat egg whites, cream of tartar and salt in large bowl until soft peaks form. Sprinkle in sugar, beating until egg whites are stiff.

5. Divide grapefruit and orange sections among four 10-ounce custard cups. Swirl top of each with meringue. Bake for 10 to 15 minutes.

Makes 4 servings. Each serving has 122 calories.

Hedgehogs

2 large apples
¼ cup honey
2 tablespoons water
1 teaspoon grated lemon rind
2 egg whites
2 tablespoons confectioners' sugar
½ cup slivered almonds

1. Preheat oven to 400° F.

2. Peel apples; cut lengthwise in half. Using teaspoon, scoop out core of each apple. Place apples cut side down in 9-inch pie plate.

3. In small saucepan, heat honey, water and lemon rind; brush over apples. Bake for 30 to 40 minutes, brushing with cooking liquid, until apples are tender. Cool completely.

4. Preheat oven to 450° F.

5. Using electric mixer at high speed, beat egg whites in medium bowl until soft peaks form; gradually add confectioners' sugar, beating until egg whites are stiff.

6. Place apple halves cut side down on cookie sheet with non-stick finish; frost apples with meringue and place 2 tablespoons slivered almonds, pincushion fashion, in meringue of each. Bake for about 5 minutes, just until meringue is browned. Serve immediately.

Makes 4 servings. Each serving has 245 calories.

Meringue Raspberry Sundaes

4 egg whites
¼ teaspoon cream of tartar
2 tablespoons sugar
1 pint vanilla ice milk
one 10-ounce package frozen raspberries, thawed

1. Preheat oven to 250° F. Line cookie sheet with brown paper.

2. Using electric mixer at high speed, beat egg whites and cream of tartar in large bowl until foamy. Add sugar, 1 tablespoon at a time; beat after each addition until soft peaks form. Fill pastry bag with meringue and press out onto paper-lined cookie sheet in 6 round shells 4 inches in diameter and 1 inch high; form a solid base first, then build up sides. Or shape shells by mounding meringue into 6 piles on paper-lined cookie sheet and, using back of wet teaspoon, make a hollow in center of each.

3. Bake for 1½ hours; cool completely. Using sharp-edged spatula, carefully remove meringue shells from paper-lined cookie sheet to wire rack.

4. To serve, fill each meringue shell with ⅓ cup ice milk; top with raspberries.

Makes 6 servings. Each serving has 140 calories.

Applesauce Pie

one 10-ounce package
    piecrust mix
2 eggs
½ cup skim milk
½ cup granulated sugar
    replacement
1 teaspoon cornstarch
½ teaspoon cinnamon
1½ cups unsweetened
    applesauce

1. Preheat oven to 425° F.

2. Prepare piecrust mix according to label directions. Divide in half; wrap and refrigerate one portion for another use. Roll out remaining half to line 8-inch pie plate. Trim and flute edge of pastry.

3. Using electric mixer at medium speed, beat eggs and skim milk in large bowl until foamy. Blend sugar replacement with cornstarch and cinnamon; beat into egg mixture. Then stir in applesauce.

4. Pour mixture into pie shell; bake for 10 minutes. Reduce oven heat to 350° F; bake 40 to 50 minutes longer or until knife inserted in center comes out clean. Cool completely.

Makes 10 servings. Each serving has 120 calories.

CalorieSaving Tip: Half a cup of unsweetened applesauce contains only two-thirds the quantity of calories in a medium apple. Make your own by steaming or pressure-cooking whole cored apples until tender and pureeing them through a sieve or food mill. Steaming the apples rather than cooking them in water gives maximum flavor to the applesauce—a real plus if you're on a diet.

Chantilly Fruit Tart

CRUST

⅔ cup vanilla wafer crumbs
½ teaspoon instant coffee
2 tablespoons diet margarine, melted

FILLING

3 tablespoons cornstarch
3 tablespoons sugar
2 cups skim milk
½ teaspoon vanilla extract

TOPPING

1 cup fresh strawberries, hulled, washed and sliced
1 cup fresh or frozen blueberries
2 tablespoons water
2 tablespoons honey

1. Preheat oven to 375° F.

2. To make crust, combine vanilla wafer crumbs, instant coffee and melted diet margarine in small bowl. Press into 8-inch pie plate to coat bottom and sides. Bake for 5 minutes; cool on wire rack. Reduce oven heat to 250° F.

3. To make filling, combine cornstarch, sugar and skim milk in small saucepan. Bring to boiling point over medium heat, stirring constantly until thickened. Cool to room temperature. Add vanilla extract and pour mixture into pie shell.

4. Meanwhile, make topping by combining strawberries, blueberries, water and honey in small saucepan. Simmer, covered, until mixture is very hot and fruit is just tender.

5. Remove fruit from liquid with slotted spoon; spoon over top of pie. Bake for 10 minutes. Serve warm.

Makes 8 servings. Each serving has 120 calories.

Coconut Custard Pie

one 10-ounce package piecrust mix
1 cup granulated sugar replacement
1 tablespoon cornstarch
2 cups skim milk
2 eggs
1 tablespoon diet margarine
1 teaspoon vanilla extract
¼ cup shredded coconut

1. Preheat oven to 375° F.

2. Prepare piecrust mix according to label directions. Divide in half; wrap and refrigerate one portion for another use. Roll out remaining half to line 8-inch pie plate. Trim and flute edge of pastry.

3. In large bowl, blend sugar replacement with cornstarch. Slowly blend in skim milk; add eggs, diet margarine and vanilla extract. Using electric mixer at medium speed, beat until smooth; stir in coconut. Pour into pastry shell; bake for 40 to 50 minutes or until knife inserted in center comes out clean. Cool completely.

Makes 10 servings. Each serving has 101 calories.

Open-Face Nectarine Pie

one 10-ounce package
piecrust mix

6 cups sliced peeled
nectarines

2 tablespoons cornstarch

¼ teaspoon cloves

¼ cup honey

2 tablespoons diet margarine

1. Preheat oven to 400° F.

2. Prepare piecrust mix according to label directions. Divide in half; wrap and refrigerate one portion for another use. Roll out remaining half to line 8-inch pie plate. Trim and flute edge of pastry. Prick pie shell well; chill or freeze for 15 minutes.

3. Meanwhile, toss nectarine slices with cornstarch and cloves. Arrange nectarines in pie shell; drizzle with honey and dot with diet margarine. Bake for 30 to 40 minutes or until nectarines are tender; let stand for 10 minutes before serving.

Makes 8 servings. Each serving has 201 calories.

Peaches and Cream Pie

one 10-ounce package pie-
crust mix

5 medium peaches, peeled
and sliced, or 4 cups frozen
unsweetened peach slices,
thawed

¼ cup granulated sugar
replacement

2 tablespoons flour

1 teaspoon grated lemon rind

¾ cup lowfat unflavored
yogurt

½ teaspoon cinnamon

1. Preheat oven to 425° F.

2. Prepare piecrust mix according to label directions. Divide in half; wrap and refrigerate one portion for another use. Roll out remaining half to line 8-inch pie plate. Trim and flute edge of pastry.

3. In large bowl, toss together peaches, sugar replacement, flour and lemon rind. Place mixture in pie shell.

4. Spread yogurt over peach mixture; sprinkle with cinnamon. Bake for 40 to 50 minutes, until pastry is golden brown and peaches are tender. Cool to room temperature before cutting.

Makes 8 servings. Each serving has 112 calories.

CalorieSaving Tip: Nectarines and peaches are among the lowest-calorie fruits of high summer. Look for them in June and July. For even fewer calories, substitute the same volume of sliced fresh strawberries and cut the cooking time in half.

Pear, Nut and Raisin Pie

one 10-ounce package
  piecrust mix
5 cups sliced, pared pears
1 tablespoon flour
2 tablespoons lemon juice
¼ cup chopped golden raisins
¼ cup chopped cashews
1 teaspoon grated lemon rind
½ teaspoon cinnamon

1. Preheat oven to 400° F.

2. Prepare piecrust mix according to label directions. Divide in half; wrap and refrigerate one portion for another use. Roll out remaining half to line 8-inch pie plate. Trim and flute edge of pastry. Prick pie shell well; chill or freeze for 15 minutes.

3. Meanwhile, toss together pear slices and flour; sprinkle pears with lemon juice. Gently combine with raisins, nuts, lemon rind and cinnamon; spoon into pie shell.

4. Bake for 30 to 35 minutes or until crust is brown and pears are tender. Let stand for 10 minutes before serving.

Makes 8 servings. Each serving has 213 calories.

Strawberry Meringue Pie

4 cups sliced fresh strawberries
⅓ cup grape juice
3 egg whites
⅛ teaspoon cream of tartar
⅛ teaspoon salt
2 tablespoons sugar

1. Preheat oven to 325° F.

2. Place strawberries in 9-inch pie plate; sprinkle with grape juice.

3. Using electric mixer at high speed, beat egg whites, cream of tartar and salt in large bowl until soft peaks form. Sprinkle in sugar, 1 tablespoon at a time; beat after each addition until egg whites are stiff.

4. Swirl meringue over strawberries. Bake for 35 to 40 minutes or until lightly browned.

Makes 4 servings. Each serving has 102 calories.

Cream Puffs

Cream Filling (recipe below)
½ cup water
¼ cup diet margarine
¼ cup flour
3 eggs

1. Prepare Cream Filling; chill. Preheat oven to 375° F.

2. Heat water and diet margarine in medium saucepan over medium heat until margarine melts and water boils. Add flour all at once; beat until mixture leaves sides of pan and forms a smooth ball.

3. Remove from heat. Using electric mixer at medium speed, beat in eggs one at a time, beating after each addition until mixture is smooth.

4. Drop dough by rounded teaspoonfuls onto ungreased cookie sheet. Bake for 30 minutes or until puffed and golden brown; remove puffs to wire rack to cool.

5. To serve, slit open top of each pastry shell and spoon in Cream Filling.

Makes 24 servings. Each serving has 133 calories.

Cream Filling

1 envelope unflavored gelatin
¼ cup water
1 cup skim milk
1 tablespoon granulated sugar replacement
1 teaspoon vanilla extract
⅛ teaspoon salt

1. Sprinkle gelatin over water in small bowl; let stand for 5 minutes to soften.

2. Heat skim milk to boiling point in small saucepan over medium heat. Remove from heat; add sugar replacement, vanilla extract and salt. Stir in softened gelatin to dissolve. Chill for 30 minutes or until thick.

3. Using electric mixer at high speed, beat until frothy. Chill until ready to fill pastry; stir well just before using.

◎ *CalorieSaving Tip:* Cream puffs are a good low-calorie dessert base to have on hand. Once they're cool, wrap them in a plastic bag and freeze them. When you crave an elegant dessert, thaw them at room temperature, then fill them with a fresh fruit puree—strawberries are ideal; so is unsweetened applesauce.

Sweet Cheese Puff

½ cup water
¼ cup diet margarine
2 tablespoons sugar
⅛ teaspoon nutmeg
½ cup sifted flour
3 eggs

   FILLING

1 cup lowfat, small curd
   cottage cheese
⅓ cup honey
2 tablespoons evaporated
   skim milk
2 tablespoons lemon juice
1 teaspoon grated lemon rind

1. Preheat oven to 400° F.

2. In medium saucepan over medium heat, combine water, diet margarine, sugar and nutmeg. Heat to boiling point.

3. Add flour all at once; beat until mixture leaves sides of pan and forms a smooth ball.

4. Remove from heat. Using electric mixer at medium speed, beat in eggs one at a time, beating after each addition until mixture is smooth. Spread mixture into 9-inch circle on baking sheet with nonstick finish, making 1-inch-high rim around edge to contain filling.

5. To make filling, blend cottage cheese, honey, evaporated milk, lemon juice and lemon rind in medium bowl.

6. Spoon filling into center of shell, spreading up to the rim. Bake for 35 to 40 minutes or until puffed and brown. Set on wire rack to cool slightly; serve warm.

Makes 8 servings. Each serving has 147 calories.

Baked Custard

1½ cups skim milk
2 eggs
2 tablespoons sugar
½ teaspoon vanilla extract
freshly grated nutmeg

1. Preheat oven to 350° F.

2. Bring skim milk to boiling point in medium saucepan over medium heat; set aside.

3. Using wire whisk, beat eggs in medium bowl until light and foamy. Pour hot milk into eggs in a steady stream, beating constantly. Beat in sugar and vanilla extract. Pour mixture into four 6-ounce custard cups. Sprinkle with grated nutmeg.

4. Set custard cups in shallow baking pan. Place on oven rack. Pour boiling water into pan to depth of 1 inch. Bake for 40 minutes or until knife inserted in center of custard comes out clean.

Makes 4 servings. Each serving has 103 calories.

Pumpkin-Coconut Custards

2 eggs, slightly beaten
1 cup skim milk
¾ cup canned pumpkin
¼ cup honey
½ teaspoon vanilla extract
¼ teaspoon ginger
¼ teaspoon nutmeg
¼ cup toasted flaked coconut

1. Preheat oven to 325° F.

2. In medium bowl, beat together eggs and skim milk; add pumpkin, stirring to blend well. Stir in honey, vanilla extract, ginger and nutmeg.

3. Divide mixture among four 10-ounce custard cups or individual soufflé dishes. Set in large shallow roasting pan. Pour boiling water into pan to depth of ¾ inch.

4. Bake for 45 minutes or until knife inserted in center of custard comes out clean. Remove custards from pan. Serve warm, each sprinkled with 1 tablespoon toasted flaked coconut.

Makes 4 servings. Each serving has 159 calories.

Rice-Date Pudding

2 cups skim milk
½ cup snipped pitted dates
¼ cup uncooked long-grain rice
¼ teaspoon salt

1. Preheat oven to 350° F.

2. Combine skim milk, dates, rice and salt in 3-cup ovenproof mold, baking dish or small casserole.

3. Bake for 1 to 1¼ hours, until thickened and creamy; stir three or four times during cooking period.

Makes 4 servings. Each serving has 146 calories.

Apricot Soufflé

one 16-ounce can apricot
   halves, drained
¾ cup graham cracker
   crumbs
2 tablespoons orange juice
1 teaspoon vanilla extract
¼ teaspoon nutmeg
4 eggs, separated
¼ cup sugar

1. Preheat oven to 325° F.

2. In electric blender, puree drained apricot halves at high speed until smooth, about 10 seconds.

3. Place in medium bowl; blend in graham cracker crumbs, orange juice, vanilla extract and nutmeg. Add egg yolks one at a time, beating well after each addition.

4. Using electric mixer at high speed, beat egg whites in large bowl until soft peaks form. Add sugar, 1 tablespoon at a time; beat after each addition until egg whites are stiff.

5. Fold egg whites into apricot mixture; pour into lightly greased 1½-quart soufflé dish. Place dish in large baking pan; pour hot water into pan to depth of 1½ inches. Bake for 1 hour, until puffed and golden on top. Serve immediately.

Makes 8 servings. Each serving has 116 calories. Shown on page 66.

Lemon Puffle

4 eggs, separated
¼ cup sugar
3 tablespoons lemon juice
2 teaspoons grated lemon rind

1. Preheat oven to 350° F.

2. Using electric mixer at high speed, beat egg yolks in large bowl until thick and lemon colored. Add 2 tablespoons of the sugar and beat until thick; slowly add lemon juice and lemon rind, beating to maintain thick consistency.

3. Using electric mixer at high speed, beat egg whites in another large bowl until soft peaks form. Gradually add remaining 2 tablespoons sugar, beating until egg whites are stiff.

4. Gently fold egg whites, one third at a time, into egg yolk mixture. Spoon into 1-quart soufflé dish with nonstick finish.

5. Set soufflé dish in large shallow roasting pan; add boiling water to pan to a depth of 1 inch. Bake for 30 to 35 minutes, until soufflé is puffed, golden brown and firm on top. Serve immediately.

Makes 4 servings. Each serving has 132 calories.

Nut Soufflés

2 tablespoons butter or margarine
2 tablespoons flour
½ cup skim milk
3 tablespoons sugar
3 eggs, separated
½ teaspoon maple extract
½ teaspoon vanilla extract
½ cup finely chopped almonds

1. Preheat oven to 375° F.

2. Melt butter or margarine in small saucepan over low heat; remove from heat. Add flour and blend until smooth. Return to heat and cook for 1 minute.

3. Gradually blend in skim milk, stirring to keep mixture smooth; add sugar. Bring to boiling point, stirring constantly until mixture thickens.

4. Using electric mixer at high speed, beat egg yolks in medium bowl until thick and lemon colored. Continue beating while adding hot milk mixture, a little at a time. Fold in maple and vanilla extracts and chopped almonds.

5. Using electric mixer at high speed, beat egg whites in another medium bowl until stiff. Using rubber spatula, gently fold egg whites, one third at a time, into egg yolk mixture.

6. Divide mixture among four 1½-cup soufflé dishes. Bake for 25 to 30 minutes or until puffed and brown on top. Serve soufflés immediately.

Makes 4 servings. Each serving has 268 calories.

Plum Puffle

½ cup packaged dried pitted prunes
3 egg whites
⅛ teaspoon cream of tartar
⅛ teaspoon salt
1 tablespoon sugar

1. Preheat oven to 350° F.

2. Cook prunes according to label directions. Cool, drain and measure 1 cup. In electric blender, puree prunes at high speed until smooth, about 10 to 15 seconds.

3. Using electric mixer at high speed, beat egg whites, cream of tartar and salt in large bowl until soft peaks form. Sprinkle in sugar, beating until egg whites are stiff.

4. Using rubber spatula, gently fold pureed prunes into egg whites; carefully pour into lightly greased 1-quart baking dish. Bake for 25 to 30 minutes or until lightly browned.

Makes 4 servings. Each serving has 99 calories.

Vanilla Soufflé

¼ cup sifted all-purpose flour
2 tablespoons sugar
1½ cups skim milk
1½ teaspoons vanilla extract
2 tablespoons diet margarine
3 egg yolks, slightly beaten
4 egg whites

1. In small bowl, blend flour, sugar and ½ cup of the skim milk until smooth. Heat remaining 1 cup skim milk and the vanilla extract in medium saucepan over low heat until bubbles form around edge.

2. Slowly stir flour mixture into milk in pan; bring to boiling point, stirring constantly until thickened. Beat in diet margarine and slightly beaten egg yolks; set aside to cool.

3. Preheat oven to 350° F.

4. Using electric mixer at high speed, beat egg whites in large bowl until stiff peaks form. Using rubber spatula, fold egg whites into egg yolk mixture. Gently pour into lightly greased 1½-quart soufflé dish. Bake for 30 to 35 minutes or until puffed, golden and firm to the touch.

Makes 8 servings. Each serving has 90 calories.

Cakes and Cookies

For those who love to bake, there's something almost magical about watching raw batter or dough being transformed in the oven into a delicious, golden brown dessert. And serving a home-baked treat when you're counting calories will boost your morale immeasurably.

One serving of most of these scrumptious desserts falls below 200 calories. To ensure the lowest possible count, keep in mind these extra calorie-saving tips.

Always use nonstick cake pans and cookie sheets to eliminate the calories added by greasing and flouring cookware. When adding extravagant ingredients such as nuts, chocolate or butterscotch bits, chop them finely so that their flavor is distributed throughout the batter, making a little go a long way. And read labels carefully so you can choose the lowest-calorie version of the ingredients you need.

One slice of Brandied Apricot Cake, moist Banana Nut Cake or any of the other cakes in this chapter is a filling, flavorful treat. If you're tempted to have seconds, though, why not bake a cake when company is coming to help polish it off? When you really feel the need to indulge, you can whip up a batch of Crispy Crisps or Meringue Drops and have a binge at 15 calories each.

For once you can have your cake and eat it too.

Angel Cake

1 cup sifted cake flour
1 cup sugar
10 egg whites
1 teaspoon cream of tartar
½ teaspoon almond extract

1. Preheat oven to 375° F.

2. Sift cake flour again along with ½ cup of the sugar. Sift twice more; set aside.

3. Using electric mixer at high speed, beat egg whites and cream of tartar in large bowl until soft peaks form. Add remaining ½ cup sugar, 2 tablespoons at a time, beating until egg whites are stiff. Fold in almond extract. Sift flour mixture, ¼ cup at a time, over egg whites; using rubber spatula, gently fold flour into egg whites after each addition.

4. Spoon batter into ungreased 9-inch tube pan. Bake on lower rack of oven for 30 minutes or until cake tester inserted in center of cake comes out clean and top surface is deep golden brown.

5. Invert pan and cool cake completely. (Pan may have a special edge to prevent cake from touching counter top; if not, suspend cake by placing tube over bottle neck.)

Makes 12 servings. Each serving has 118 calories.

Apricot Angel Cake

one 16-ounce package angel food cake mix
one 8¾-ounce can apricot halves in light syrup
2 tablespoons lemon juice
1 cup vanilla ice milk
1 cup fresh blueberries or frozen blueberries, thawed

1. Prepare angel food cake according to label directions. Suspend and cool cake according to directions; remove from pan.

2. Meanwhile, puree apricot halves and lemon juice in electric blender at high speed until smooth, about 10 seconds.

3. To serve, place one-twelfth of cake on each of 4 individual dessert plates; wrap and freeze remaining cake for later use. Top each serving with ¼ cup ice milk and ¼ cup apricot sauce; sprinkle each with ¼ cup blueberries.

Makes 4 servings. Each serving has 203 calories.

Angel Fruitcake

one 16-ounce package angel
food cake mix

one 17-ounce can fruit cocktail

1 envelope unflavored gelatin

½ cup orange juice

one 8-ounce container lowfat
lemon-flavored yogurt

2 egg whites

1. Prepare angel food cake according to label directions. Suspend and cool cake according to directions; remove from pan.

2. Meanwhile, drain juice from fruit cocktail into small saucepan. Sprinkle gelatin over juice; let stand for 5 minutes to soften. Place over very low heat just until gelatin is dissolved. Stir in orange juice and yogurt; chill until semi-set, about 30 minutes.

3. Using electric mixer at high speed, beat egg whites in small bowl until stiff. Using rubber spatula, fold egg whites and fruit cocktail into gelatin mixture.

4. Cut angel food cake horizontally into 3 layers. Place bottom layer on serving platter; top with half of filling; set second layer in place and top with remaining filling and final layer. Chill cake for at least 1 hour to firm filling.

Makes 12 servings. Each serving has 186 calories.

Upside-Down Angel Cake

one 16-ounce package angel
food cake mix

one 8-ounce can pineapple
rings in natural juices

1 envelope unflavored gelatin

½ cup canned pitted water-
pack cherries

1. Prepare angel food cake according to label directions. Suspend and cool cake according to directions; remove from pan. Cut horizontally in half. Reserve top half for dessert; wrap and freeze bottom half for later use.

2. Drain juice from pineapple rings into small saucepan. Sprinkle gelatin over juice; let stand for 5 minutes to soften. Place over very low heat just until gelatin is dissolved.

3. Arrange pineapple rings on bottom of clean angel cake pan. Cut cherries in half and arrange between pineapple rings. Pour in gelatin mixture; chill until semi-set, about 20 to 30 minutes.

4. Place angel food cake in pan, pressing lightly into semi-set gelatin mixture. Chill until completely set, about 1½ hours. Dip pan quickly in hot water and unmold cake on serving platter.

Makes 12 servings. Each serving has 97 calories.

Apple Cinnamon Cake

1 cup canned unsweetened apple slices
3 eggs, separated
⅓ cup sugar
½ teaspoon cinnamon
¼ teaspoon salt
2 tablespoons water
½ cup flour
¼ teaspoon cream of tartar

1. Preheat oven to 325° F. Use 8-inch round cake pan with nonstick finish if possible; otherwise, lightly grease and flour one 8-inch cake pan. Place apple slices in pan; set aside.

2. Using electric mixer at medium speed, beat egg yolks, 3 tablespoons of the sugar, the cinnamon, salt and water in medium bowl until foamy and light in color. Gently fold in flour.

3. Using electric mixer at high speed, beat egg whites and cream of tartar in large bowl until soft peaks form. Add remaining sugar; beat 2 minutes longer.

4. Gently fold egg whites into flour mixture; pour over apple slices. Bake for 25 to 30 minutes. Cool cake in pan on wire rack for 15 minutes; unmold cake onto serving platter.

Makes 8 servings. Each serving has 87 calories.

CalorieSaving Tip: Low-calorie egg whites become a high-volume food once they're beaten; their fluffy lightness creates the illusion of greater quantity. For maximum volume, separate the eggs while they're cold, but let the egg whites reach room temperature before you begin to beat them. Be sure to place them in a clean bowl and use clean beaters. Any trace of fat (or wayward yolk) will lower the volume of the egg whites.

Apple Crisp Cake

one 20-ounce can
  unsweetened apple slices
2 teaspoons granulated sugar
  replacement
1 teaspoon cinnamon
2 eggs, separated
¼ cup sugar
1 tablespoon water
⅛ teaspoon salt
⅓ cup flour
⅛ teaspoon cream of tartar
¼ cup diet margarine, melted

1. Preheat oven to 350° F.

2. Place apple slices in 8-inch pie plate; sprinkle with mixture of sugar replacement and cinnamon.

3. Using electric mixer at high speed, beat egg yolks, 2 tablespoons of the sugar, the water and salt in medium bowl until foamy and pale. Using rubber spatula, gently fold in flour.

4. Using electric mixer at high speed, beat egg whites and cream of tartar in another medium bowl until soft peaks form. Add remaining 2 tablespoons sugar; beat 1 minute longer.

5. Using rubber spatula, gently fold egg whites into flour mixture. Spread over apples; gently pour melted diet margarine over top. Bake for 40 to 50 minutes or until golden and crisp. For very crisp topping, broil 6 inches from heat for 2 to 3 minutes. Cool cake in pan on wire rack for 15 minutes.

Makes 8 servings. Each serving has 115 calories.

Applesauce-Raisin Cake

1 cup all-purpose flour
¾ teaspoon baking soda
½ teaspoon cinnamon
¼ teaspoon salt
¼ cup diet margarine
¼ cup brown sugar, firmly
  packed
¼ cup granulated sugar
¼ cup granulated sugar
  replacement
1 egg
½ cup unsweetened
  applesauce
¼ cup golden raisins,
  chopped

1. Preheat oven to 350° F. Use 8 x 8 x 2-inch cake pan with nonstick finish if possible; otherwise, lightly grease and flour 8-inch square cake pan.

2. In medium bowl, combine flour, baking soda, cinnamon and salt; set aside.

3. Using electric mixer at low speed, beat together diet margarine, brown sugar, granulated sugar and sugar replacement in large bowl; beat in egg. Gradually stir in flour mixture. Add applesauce and chopped raisins; stir until well mixed.

4. Pour mixture into prepared pan; bake for 35 to 40 minutes, until cake tester inserted in center comes out clean. Cool completely on wire rack.

Makes 8 servings. Each serving has 124 calories.

Spicy Applesauce Cake

½ cup butter or margarine, softened
½ cup brown sugar, lightly packed
1 cup unsweetened applesauce
2 cups sifted all-purpose flour
1 teaspoon baking powder
1 teaspoon baking soda
1 teaspoon cinnamon
¼ teaspoon cloves
¼ teaspoon nutmeg

1. Preheat oven to 375° F.

2. Using electric mixer at high speed, beat together butter or margarine and brown sugar in medium bowl until light and fluffy. Add applesauce; beat to blend well.

3. Sift flour with baking powder, baking soda, cinnamon, cloves and nutmeg. Using electric mixer at low speed, gently stir flour mixture, one third at a time, into applesauce mixture. Pour into 9 x 9 x 2-inch baking pan with nonstick finish.

4. Bake for 45 to 50 minutes. Cool cake in pan on wire rack for 10 minutes; remove from pan to wire rack and cool completely. Cut into 1½-inch squares.

Makes 36 squares. Each square has 80 calories.

Brandied Apricot Cake

one 8¾-ounce can apricot halves, drained
1½ tablespoons brandy
¼ cup chopped walnuts
one 8-inch store-bought angel food cake

1. In electric blender, puree apricots at high speed until smooth, about 5 to 10 seconds.

2. In small bowl, combine apricots, brandy and walnuts. Place cake on serving platter; spoon mixture on top of cake and allow to drip down sides. Chill. Use serrated knife to cut.

Makes 12 servings. Each serving has 186 calories. If divided into 16, each serving has 140 calories.

Banana Nut Cake

1 cup all-purpose flour
⅔ cup sugar
½ cup granulated sugar
   replacement
2 teaspoons baking powder
½ teaspoon baking soda
2 eggs
½ cup vegetable oil
1 medium banana, mashed
¼ cup chopped walnuts

1. Preheat oven to 350° F. Use 8 x 8 x 2-inch cake pan with nonstick finish if possible; otherwise, lightly grease and flour one 8-inch square cake pan.

2. In large bowl, combine flour, sugar, sugar replacement, baking powder and baking soda. Add eggs, oil and banana; using electric mixer at medium speed, beat until smooth. Stir in chopped walnuts.

3. Pour mixture into prepared pan; bake for 30 to 40 minutes, until cake tester inserted in center comes out clean. Cool cake in pan on wire rack for 5 minutes; remove from pan to wire rack and cool completely.

Makes 12 servings. Each serving has 172 calories.

Blueberry Cupcakes

3 eggs, separated
⅓ cup sugar
2 tablespoons water
¼ teaspoon salt
½ cup flour
½ cup frozen unsweetened
   blueberries, thawed
¼ teaspoon cream of tartar

1. Preheat oven to 325° F. Use 12 muffin cups with nonstick finish or line muffin cups with paper liners.

2. Using electric mixer at high speed, beat egg yolks, 3 tablespoons of the sugar, the water and salt in large bowl until foamy and light in color. Using rubber spatula, gently fold in flour and blueberries.

3. Using electric mixer at high speed, beat egg whites and cream of tartar in another large bowl until soft peaks form. Add remaining sugar; beat 2 minutes longer.

4. Using rubber spatula, gently fold egg whites into blueberry mixture; fill muffin cups two-thirds full. Bake for 20 to 25 minutes or until golden brown. Remove from cups to wire rack to cool.

Makes 12 cupcakes. Each cupcake has 61 calories.

Orange Cake

1 cup all-purpose flour

⅓ cup sugar

⅓ cup granulated sugar replacement

2 tablespoons grated orange rind

2 teaspoons baking powder

¼ teaspoon salt

2 eggs

½ cup vegetable oil

3 tablespoons fresh orange juice

2 teaspoons lemon juice

1. Preheat oven to 375° F. Use 8 x 8 x 2-inch cake pan with nonstick finish if possible; otherwise, lightly grease and flour one 8-inch square cake pan.

2. In large bowl, combine flour, sugar, sugar replacement, orange rind, baking powder and salt. Add eggs, oil, orange juice and lemon juice; using electric mixer at medium speed, beat until smooth.

3. Pour mixture into prepared pan; bake for 35 to 40 minutes, until cake tester inserted in center comes out clean. Cool cake in pan on wire rack for 5 minutes; remove from pan to wire rack and cool completely.

Makes 12 servings. Each serving has 132 calories.

Orange Chiffon Cake

1 cup sifted cake flour

⅓ cup sugar

1½ teaspoons baking powder

¼ teaspoon salt

2 egg yolks

2 tablespoons vegetable oil

⅓ cup orange juice

1 tablespoon grated orange rind

4 egg whites

¼ teaspoon cream of tartar

1. Preheat oven to 325° F.

2. Sift cake flour again along with sugar, baking powder and salt into large bowl. Make a well in center of mixture; add egg yolks, oil, orange juice and orange rind. Using electric mixer at low speed, beat until smooth.

3. Using electric mixer at high speed, beat egg whites and cream of tartar in another large bowl until egg whites are stiff. Using rubber spatula, gently fold egg whites, one third at a time, into egg yolk batter just until combined. Spoon mixture into 9-inch tube pan.

4. Bake for 50 minutes or until cake tester inserted in center comes out clean. Invert pan immediately and cool cake completely. (Pan may have a special edge to prevent cake from touching counter top; if not, suspend cake by placing tube over bottle neck.)

Makes 12 servings. Each serving has 90 calories.

Peach Topsy-Turvy Cake

one 8-ounce can sliced
  peaches
1 tablespoon brown sugar
3 eggs, separated
1/3 cup granulated sugar
2 tablespoons water
1/4 teaspoon salt
1/2 cup flour
1/4 teaspoon cream of tartar

1. Preheat oven to 350° F. Use 8 x 8 x 2-inch cake pan with nonstick finish if possible; otherwise, lightly grease and flour one 8-inch square pan.

2. Drain and rinse peach slices; pat dry with paper towels. Place peach slices in bottom of prepared cake pan. Sprinkle with brown sugar.

3. Using electric mixer at high speed, beat egg yolks, 1/4 cup of the granulated sugar, the water and salt in medium bowl until foamy and light in color. Using rubber spatula, gently fold in the flour.

4. Using electric mixer at high speed, beat egg whites and cream of tartar in large bowl until soft peaks form. Add remaining granulated sugar; beat 2 minutes longer. Using rubber spatula, gently fold egg whites into flour mixture.

5. Spread mixture over peaches to cover. Bake for 30 to 35 minutes, until cake tester inserted in center comes out clean. Cool cake in pan on wire rack for 15 minutes. Unmold onto serving platter; cut into 2 1/4-inch squares.

Makes 8 servings. Each serving has 92 calories. Shown on page 67.

🛟 *CalorieSaving Tip:* Beaten egg whites, the dieter's boon, hold their volume when sugar is slowly beaten into them. Add no more than 1 tablespoon at a time to the whites, and beat well after each addition so the sugar is thoroughly absorbed. You'll need less sugar if you first beat the whites with a little salt or cream of tartar. As long as you own a rubber spatula, there's no mystique to folding the beaten whites into any mixture. With the edge of the spatula, gently scoop under the mixture and cut across the top surface, rotating the bowl a quarter turn after each fold. The object is to fold just until the whites are blended into the mixture—don't overdo it!

Almond Bars

¾ cup butter or margarine, softened

⅓ cup sugar

½ teaspoon almond extract

2 cups sifted all-purpose flour

1. Using electric mixer at high speed, beat together butter or margarine, sugar and almond extract in medium bowl until light and fluffy. With mixer at low speed, gently stir in flour just until blended.

2. Roll dough into 14 x 7-inch rectangle directly onto cookie sheet with nonstick finish. Crimp edge of dough to form decorative design; using sharp knife, mark into 2¼ x ½-inch rectangles. Chill for 15 minutes.

3. Preheat oven to 325° F.

4. Bake for 40 minutes or until crisp. Cut into bars where marked; cool completely on cookie sheet on wire rack.

Makes 84 bars. Each bar has 43 calories.

Almond Center Cookies

½ cup diet margarine

½ cup granulated sugar replacement

¼ teaspoon almond extract

1 cup sifted all-purpose flour

⅛ teaspoon baking powder

⅛ teaspoon salt

9 whole blanched almonds

1. Preheat oven to 375° F.

2. Using electric mixer at high speed, beat together diet margarine and sugar replacement in medium bowl until creamy; beat in almond extract. With mixer at low speed, stir in sifted flour, baking powder and salt; blend thoroughly.

3. Roll dough into ¾-inch balls; place 1½ inches apart on cookie sheet with nonstick finish. Flatten each ball with bottom of floured glass.

4. Split each almond in half; press into center of each cookie. Bake for 10 to 12 minutes. Remove cookies to wire rack to cool.

Makes 18 cookies. Each cookie has 54 calories.

Applesauce Spice Cookies

½ cup diet margarine

½ cup brown sugar, firmly packed

¼ cup unsweetened applesauce

¼ teaspoon vanilla extract

2¼ cups sifted all-purpose flour

¼ teaspoon baking soda

¼ teaspoon cinnamon

¼ teaspoon nutmeg

⅛ teaspoon cloves

¼ cup golden raisins, chopped

1. Preheat oven to 375° F.

2. Using electric mixer at high speed, beat together diet margarine and brown sugar in large bowl until creamy; beat in applesauce and vanilla extract.

3. In separate bowl, sift flour again along with baking soda, cinnamon, nutmeg and cloves. With mixer at low speed, slowly stir flour mixture into applesauce mixture. Stir in chopped raisins, mixing well.

4. Drop dough by rounded teaspoonfuls 1½ inches apart onto cookie sheet with nonstick finish. Bake for 10 to 12 minutes. Remove cookies to wire rack to cool.

Makes 20 cookies. Each cookie has 74 calories.

Apricot Chocolatey Cookies

2 egg whites

¼ teaspoon salt

¼ teaspoon almond extract

2 tablespoons sugar

2 cups cocoa-flavored sweetened puffed-rice cereal

¼ cup finely chopped dried apricots

1. Preheat oven to 350° F.

2. Using electric mixer at high speed, beat egg whites and salt in large bowl until foamy. Add almond extract; beat 30 seconds longer.

3. Add sugar, 1 tablespoon at a time; beat after each addition until soft peaks form.

4. Using rubber spatula, gently fold cocoa-flavored cereal and apricots into meringue mixture. Make mounds of 2 teaspoons each on cookie sheet with nonstick finish.

5. Bake for 10 to 12 minutes; cool slightly. Remove cookies to wire rack to cool completely.

Makes 18 cookies. Each cookie has 26 calories.

Butterscotchies

⅓ cup diet margarine

⅓ cup brown sugar, firmly packed

¼ teaspoon vanilla extract

1 cup sifted all-purpose flour

⅛ teaspoon baking powder

⅛ teaspoon salt

2 tablespoons butterscotch morsels, finely chopped

1. Using electric mixer at high speed, beat together diet margarine and sugar in medium bowl until creamy; beat in vanilla extract. With mixer at low speed, stir in sifted flour, baking powder and salt; blend thoroughly.

2. Form into roll, 1½ inches in diameter; wrap in waxed paper or plastic wrap. Chill for at least 8 hours or overnight.

3. Preheat oven to 400° F.

4. Cut cookie roll into ¼-inch slices. Place on cookie sheet with nonstick finish. Sprinkle with chopped butterscotch morsels. Bake for 8 to 10 minutes. Remove cookies to wire rack to cool.

Makes 20 cookies. Each cookie has 53 calories.

Cinnamon Cookies

⅓ cup diet margarine

⅓ cup granulated sugar replacement

1 egg

½ teaspoon vanilla extract

1¼ cups sifted all-purpose flour

½ teaspoon grated lemon rind

¼ teaspoon salt

1 tablespoon sugar

1 teaspoon cinnamon

1. Preheat oven to 375° F.

2. Using electric mixer at high speed, beat together diet margarine and sugar replacement in medium bowl until creamy; beat in egg and vanilla extract. With mixer at low speed, stir in sifted flour, lemon rind and salt; mix well.

3. Roll half of dough directly onto cookie sheet with nonstick finish to ⅛-inch thickness. Cut into 2-inch cookies with a cutter. Remove surplus dough. Sprinkle cookies with a little sugar-cinnamon mixture. Bake for 8 to 10 minutes. Remove cookies to wire rack to cool. Repeat to use all dough.

Makes 24 cookies. Each cookie has 41 calories.

Crispy Crisps

2 egg whites
¼ teaspoon salt
¼ teaspoon vanilla extract
2 tablespoons sugar
2 cups unsweetened puffed-
  rice cereal

1. Preheat oven to 325° F.

2. Using electric mixer at high speed, beat egg whites and salt in large bowl until foamy. Add vanilla extract; beat 30 seconds longer.

3. Add sugar, 1 tablespoon at a time; beat after each addition until soft peaks form.

4. Using rubber spatula, gently fold puffed-rice cereal into meringue mixture. Make mounds of 2 teaspoons each on cookie sheet with nonstick finish.

5. Bake for 15 minutes; cool slightly. Using sharp-edged spatula, remove cookies to wire rack to cool completely.

Makes 18 cookies. Each cookie has 15 calories.

Date Bars

½ cup diet margarine
¼ cup brown sugar, firmly
  packed
1 cup snipped dates
½ cup sifted all-purpose flour
½ cup quick-cooking oats
¼ teaspoon baking powder
¼ teaspoon salt

1. Preheat oven to 350° F.

2. Using electric mixer at high speed, beat together diet margarine and brown sugar in medium bowl until creamy. With mixer at low speed, stir in dates. Blend in sifted flour, oats, baking powder and salt; stir to mix well.

3. Line bottom of 8 x 8 x 2-inch baking pan with waxed paper; spread mixture in pan. Bake for 30 to 35 minutes. Cool in pan on wire rack.

Makes 16 bars. Each bar has 88 calories.

Note: For best results, use wet scissors to snip dates.

Icebox Cream Cheese Cookies

⅓ cup diet margarine

half of 3-ounce package imitation cream cheese

½ cup granulated sugar replacement

¼ teaspoon vanilla extract

1 cup sifted all-purpose flour

⅛ teaspoon baking powder

⅛ teaspoon salt

1. Using electric mixer at high speed, beat together diet margarine, imitation cream cheese and granulated sugar replacement in medium bowl until creamy; beat in vanilla extract. With mixer at low speed, stir in sifted flour along with baking powder and salt.

2. Form into roll, 1½ inches in diameter; wrap in waxed paper or plastic wrap. Chill for at least 8 hours or overnight.

3. Preheat oven to 400° F.

4. Cut cookie roll into ¼-inch slices. Place on cookie sheet with nonstick finish. Bake for 8 to 10 minutes. Remove cookies to wire rack to cool.

Makes 20 cookies. Each cookie has 40 calories.

Meringue Drops

4 egg whites

¼ teaspoon cream of tartar

2 tablespoons sugar

½ cup chopped walnuts

1. Preheat oven to 250° F. Line cookie sheet with brown paper.

2. Using electric mixer at high speed, beat egg whites and cream of tartar in large bowl until foamy. Add sugar, 1 tablespoon at a time; beat after each addition until the egg whites are stiff.

3. Using rubber spatula, gently fold walnuts into meringue mixture. Drop by heaping teaspoonfuls onto paper-lined cookie sheet.

4. Bake for 1 hour; cool slightly. Using sharp-edged spatula, remove meringues from paper-lined cookie sheet to wire rack to cool completely.

Makes 36 drops. Each drop has 15 calories.

Mocha Cookies

½ cup diet margarine

¼ cup granulated sugar replacement

¼ cup brown sugar, firmly packed

¼ teaspoon vanilla extract

1 cup sifted all-purpose flour

2 tablespoons cocoa powder

1 teaspoon instant coffee

⅛ teaspoon baking powder

⅛ teaspoon salt

1. Preheat oven to 375° F.

2. Using electric mixer at high speed, beat together diet margarine, sugar replacement and brown sugar in medium bowl until creamy; beat in vanilla extract. With mixer at low speed, stir in sifted flour, cocoa, instant coffee, baking powder and salt; blend thoroughly.

3. Drop dough by rounded teaspoonfuls 1½ inches apart onto cookie sheet with nonstick finish. Bake for 10 to 12 minutes. Remove cookies to wire rack to cool.

Makes 24 cookies. Each cookie has 37 calories.

Spiced Mocha Crisps

1½ cups sifted all-purpose flour

2 teaspoons baking powder

2 teaspoons instant coffee

¼ teaspoon cinnamon

¼ teaspoon ground cloves

2 tablespoons diet margarine

½ cup sugar

1 egg

¼ cup carob powder or cocoa powder

1. Sift flour again along with baking powder, instant coffee, cinnamon and cloves. Set aside.

2. Using electric mixer at high speed, beat together diet margarine, sugar and egg in medium bowl. With mixer at low speed, blend in carob or cocoa powder, then blend in flour mixture. Wrap dough in plastic wrap; chill dough until firm, at least 1 hour.

3. Preheat oven to 350° F.

4. Roll half of dough directly onto cookie sheet with nonstick finish to ⅛-inch thickness. Cut into 2-inch cookies with a cutter. Remove surplus dough. Bake for 8 to 10 minutes. Remove cookies to wire rack to cool. Repeat to use all dough.

Makes 30 cookies. Each cookie has 41 calories.

Spice Cookies

¼ cup diet margarine

⅓ cup granulated sugar replacement

1 egg

½ teaspoon vanilla extract

1 cup sifted all-purpose flour

½ teaspoon cinnamon

½ teaspoon ginger

¼ teaspoon salt

1. Preheat oven to 350° F.

2. Using electric mixer at high speed, beat together diet margarine and sugar replacement in medium bowl until creamy; beat in egg and vanilla extract. With mixer at low speed, stir in sifted flour, cinnamon, ginger and salt; blend well.

3. Roll half of dough directly onto cookie sheet with nonstick finish to ⅛-inch thickness. Cut into 2-inch cookies with a cutter. Remove surplus dough. Bake for 8 to 10 minutes. Cool cookies on cookie sheet for 2 minutes; remove to wire rack to cool completely. Repeat to use all dough.

Makes 24 cookies. Each cookie has 31 calories

Coconut Oatmeal Cookies

½ cup diet margarine

⅓ cup granulated sugar replacement

⅓ cup brown sugar, firmly packed

¼ teaspoon vanilla extract

½ cup sifted all-purpose flour

½ cup quick-cooking oats

¼ cup shredded coconut

¼ teaspoon baking soda

⅛ teaspoon baking powder

⅛ teaspoon salt

1. Preheat oven to 375° F.

2. Using electric mixer at high speed, beat together diet margarine, sugar replacement and brown sugar in medium bowl until creamy; beat in vanilla extract. With mixer at low speed, stir in sifted flour, oats, coconut, baking soda, baking powder and salt; mix well.

3. Drop dough by rounded teaspoonfuls 1½ inches apart onto cookie sheet with nonstick finish. Bake for 10 to 12 minutes. Cool cookies on cookie sheet for 2 minutes; remove to wire rack to cool completely.

Makes 24 cookies. Each cookie has 50 calories.

Oatmeal Fairings

½ cup diet margarine
¼ cup granulated sugar replacement
¼ cup brown sugar, firmly packed
2 teaspoons water
½ teaspoon vanilla extract
½ cup sifted all-purpose flour
½ cup quick-cooking oats
¼ teaspoon baking soda
⅛ teaspoon salt

1. Preheat oven to 350° F.

2. Using electric mixer at high speed, beat together diet margarine, sugar replacement and brown sugar in medium bowl until creamy; beat in water and vanilla extract. With mixer at low speed, stir in sifted flour, oats, baking soda and salt; blend thoroughly.

3. Drop dough by rounded teaspoonfuls 2 inches apart onto cookie sheet with nonstick finish. Bake for 10 to 12 minutes. Remove cookies to wire rack to cool.

Makes 18 cookies. Each cookie has 53 calories.

Orange-Coconut Crisps

½ cup diet margarine
½ cup granulated sugar replacement
¼ cup shredded coconut
1 teaspoon grated orange rind
½ teaspoon orange juice
1 cup sifted all-purpose flour
⅛ teaspoon baking powder
⅛ teaspoon salt

1. Preheat oven to 375° F.

2. Using electric mixer at high speed, beat together diet margarine and sugar replacement in medium bowl until creamy.

3. With mixer at low speed, stir in coconut, orange rind and orange juice; blend well. Stir in sifted flour, baking powder and salt; blend thoroughly.

4. Drop dough by rounded teaspoonfuls 1½ inches apart onto cookie sheet with nonstick finish. Bake for 10 to 12 minutes. Remove cookies to wire rack to cool.

Makes 24 cookies. Each cookie has 43 calories.

Orange Cream Cheese Cookies

½ cup diet margarine

half of 3-ounce package imitation cream cheese

½ cup granulated sugar replacement

½ teaspoon grated orange rind

½ teaspoon orange juice

1 cup sifted all-purpose flour

⅛ teaspoon baking powder

⅛ teaspoon salt

1. Preheat oven to 375° F.

2. Using electric mixer at high speed, beat together diet margarine, imitation cream cheese and sugar replacement in medium bowl until creamy; beat in orange rind and orange juice. With mixer at low speed, stir in sifted flour along with baking powder and salt.

3. Roll dough into 1-inch balls; place 1½ inches apart on cookie sheet with nonstick finish. Flatten each ball with bottom of floured glass. Bake for 10 to 12 minutes. Remove cookies to wire rack to cool.

Makes 24 cookies. Each cookie has 39 calories.

Orange Wafers

½ cup butter or margarine, softened

⅓ cup sugar

1 tablespoon orange juice

2 teaspoons grated orange rind

1 cup sifted all-purpose flour

3 egg whites

1. Preheat oven to 400° F.

2. Using electric mixer at high speed, beat together butter or margarine, sugar, orange juice and orange rind in medium bowl until light and fluffy. With mixer at low speed, gently stir in flour alternately with unbeaten egg whites, making sure both are absorbed after each addition.

3. Drop batter by teaspoonfuls 1 inch apart on cookie sheet with nonstick finish. Bake for 10 minutes or until edges are browned. Cool on cookie sheet for 1 minute; using small sharp-edged spatula, remove cookies to wire rack to cool.

Makes 42 cookies. Each wafer has 57 calories.

Peanut Butter Cookies

½ cup diet margarine
¼ cup granulated sugar replacement
¼ cup brown sugar, firmly packed
¼ cup creamy peanut butter
1 cup sifted all-purpose flour
¼ teaspoon baking soda
⅛ teaspoon salt

1. Preheat oven to 375° F.

2. Using electric mixer at high speed, beat together diet margarine, sugar replacement, brown sugar and peanut butter in medium bowl until creamy. With mixer at low speed, stir in sifted flour, baking soda and salt; blend thoroughly.

3. Roll dough into 1-inch balls; place 2 inches apart on cookie sheet with nonstick finish. Using fork dipped in flour, flatten each ball in a crisscross pattern. Bake for 10 to 12 minutes. Remove cookies to wire rack to cool.

Makes 20 cookies. Each cookie has 71 calories.

Pecan Crisps

½ cup diet margarine
⅓ cup brown sugar, firmly packed
¼ teaspoon vanilla extract
1 cup sifted all-purpose flour
⅛ teaspoon salt
1 egg white, slightly beaten
½ cup finely chopped pecans

1. Preheat oven to 375° F.

2. Using electric mixer at high speed, beat together diet margarine and brown sugar in medium bowl until creamy; beat in vanilla extract. With mixer at low speed, stir in sifted flour and salt; blend thoroughly.

3. Roll dough into 1-inch balls. Dip each ball into slightly beaten egg white, then roll in chopped pecans to coat. Place balls 1 inch apart on cookie sheet with nonstick finish. Bake for 10 to 12 minutes. Remove cookies to wire rack to cool.

Makes 18 cookies. Each cookie has 58 calories.

Summer Fruit Bowl with Yogurt (*page 26*)

Apricot Soufflé (*page 42*)

Topsy-Turvy Peach Cake (*page 54*)

Hot Chocolate Alexander (*page 85*)

Chocolate-Mint Chiffon Pie (*page 89*)

Orange-Lemon Mousse (*page 98*)

Strawberry Shortcake (*page 132*)

Cherries Jubilee (*page 124*)

Spritz Cookies

½ cup diet margarine
⅓ cup granulated sugar replacement
1 egg yolk
¼ teaspoon vanilla extract
1¼ cups sifted all-purpose flour
⅛ teaspoon salt

1. Preheat oven to 375° F.

2. Using electric mixer at high speed, beat together diet margarine and sugar replacement in medium bowl until creamy; beat in egg yolk and vanilla extract. With mixer at low speed, stir in sifted flour and salt.

3. Fill cookie press with half of dough; press 1½-inch-diameter cookies directly onto cookie sheet with nonstick finish. Bake for 8 to 10 minutes. Remove cookies to wire rack to cool.

Makes 30 cookies. Each cookie has 34 calories.

Chocolate Spritz Cookies

1 recipe Spritz Cookies (see above)
two 1-ounce squares semisweet chocolate

1. Prepare Spritz Cookies. Place chocolate squares in small custard cup; set in small saucepan containing 1 inch water. Melt chocolate over low heat, stirring constantly; remove from heat.

2. Dip Spritz Cookies in melted chocolate to coat one half of each. Place cookies on wire rack over waxed paper to catch chocolate drippings.

Makes 30 cookies. Each cookie has 43 calories.

CalorieSaving Tip: By using a cookie press, you avoid rolling your cookie dough on a floured board or a greased cookie sheet; thus you cut a number of calories per batch of cookies. No cookie press? Divide the dough for the Spritz Cookies (above) into 30 pieces; place the pieces on a cookie sheet with a nonstick surface and press each piece with the bottom of a glass that's been dipped in water. Each piece of dough should be 1½ inches in diameter. Bake all these low-calorie cookies as you would their higher-calorie counterparts —until they're golden around the edges. Overbaking destroys the flavor of any cookie.

Vanilla Jelly Cookies

½ cup diet margarine
⅓ cup granulated sugar replacement
½ teaspoon vanilla extract
1 cup sifted all-purpose flour
⅛ teaspoon baking powder
⅛ teaspoon salt
4 teaspoons currant jelly

1. Preheat oven to 400° F.

2. Using electric mixer at high speed, beat together diet margarine and sugar replacement in medium bowl until creamy; beat in vanilla extract. With mixer at low speed, stir in sifted flour, baking powder and salt; blend well.

3. Roll dough into 1-inch balls; place 1½ inches apart on cookie sheet with nonstick finish. Slightly flatten each ball with bottom of floured glass.

4. Make slight depression with tip of little finger in center of each cookie; fill each with ¼ teaspoon currant jelly. Bake for 10 to 12 minutes. Remove cookies to wire rack to cool.

Makes 16 cookies. Each cookie has 60 calories.

Walnutties

⅓ cup diet margarine
⅓ cup granulated sugar replacement
1 teaspoon orange juice
½ teaspoon vanilla extract
½ teaspoon grated lemon rind
1 cup sifted all-purpose flour
¼ teaspoon baking powder
⅓ cup chopped walnuts

1. Using electric mixer at high speed, beat diet margarine and sugar replacement in medium bowl until creamy; beat in orange juice, vanilla extract and lemon rind. With mixer at low speed, stir in sifted flour and baking powder; blend thoroughly. Stir in chopped walnuts.

2. Form into roll, 1½ inches in diameter; wrap in waxed paper or plastic wrap. Chill for at least 8 hours or overnight.

3. Preheat oven to 400° F.

4. Cut cookie roll into ¼-inch slices. Place on cookie sheet with nonstick finish. Bake for 8 to 10 minutes. Remove cookies to wire rack to cool.

Makes 20 cookies. Each cookie has 46 calories.

Chocolate Confections

Chocolate. Even the word sounds rich, laden with memories of velvety mousses, moist, dark cakes, spoon-licking puddings, finger-smudging candy. Ask any dessert lover his or her single favorite flavor, and 9 out of 10 times the answer is: chocolate.

If your mouth is watering at the very mention of the word and guilt is creeping up your backbone as you contemplate an all-out caloric revolt, read on, because a solution is at hand. Almost two dozen solutions, in fact. The richest of our chocolate recipes contains under 250 calories a serving, and most are well below that.

Real, rich chocolate, full of cocoa butter, can be devastating to a diet, so adhere strictly to the quantities specified in the recipes. You'll love the results — Pots de Crème au Chocolat, Baked Chocolate Custard, Chocolate Cake and Chocolate Chip Cookies, for instance.

As you make these recipes, remember that chocolate scorches easily. To prevent burning, melt it slowly over very low heat in a double boiler or with other liquids. Cocoa is also used in these recipes, with the option of substituting carob, a natural chocolate alternative that is not as bitter as cocoa. Both are powders and must be mixed thoroughly with liquids to avoid dry pockets in the batter.

Chocolate Bavarian Cream, Chocolate-Mint Angel Cake, Chocolate Cheese Pie — getting hungry? Just turn the page.

Chocolate Bavarian

1 envelope unflavored gelatin
¼ cup water
1¾ cups skim milk
⅓ cup carob powder or
  cocoa powder
¼ cup sugar
1 teaspoon vanilla extract
¼ teaspoon almond extract
2 cups Low-Calorie Whipped
  Topping (see page 93)

1. Sprinkle gelatin over water in small custard cup; let stand for 5 minutes to soften.

2. In small saucepan, blend skim milk, carob or cocoa powder and sugar; heat, stirring constantly, until sugar dissolves and mixture bubbles around edge.

3. Remove from heat; stir in softened gelatin, vanilla and almond extracts. Pour into medium bowl; cool, then chill until semi-set, at least 1 hour.

4. Using electric mixer at high speed, beat gelatin mixture until fluffy. Using rubber spatula, gently fold in whipped topping. Spoon into 1-quart mold; chill until completely set, at least 1 hour.

5. Dip mold into hot water and invert onto serving platter; shake to release mold.

Makes 8 servings. Each serving has 93 calories.

Frozen Chocolate Custard

1⅔ cups skim milk
¼ cup flour
¼ cup sugar
1 tablespoon carob powder or
  cocoa powder
1 teaspoon vanilla extract

1. Heat skim milk in small saucepan over medium heat until bubbles form at edge. In medium bowl, combine flour, sugar, carob or cocoa powder and vanilla extract; beat in hot milk, keeping mixture smooth.

2. Return mixture to saucepan; bring to boiling point, stirring constantly. Pour into 1-quart mold; cool, then freeze until firm.

Makes 4 servings. Each serving has 104 calories.

Taste of Chocolate Custard

4 egg yolks, beaten
¼ cup sugar
2 cups skim milk
1 teaspoon vanilla extract
1 tablespoon chocolate sprinkles

1. In medium bowl, thoroughly blend beaten egg yolks and sugar. Heat skim milk in medium saucepan over medium heat until bubbles form around edge.

2. Rapidly stir hot milk into egg yolk mixture, then return mixture to saucepan. Cook over very low heat, stirring constantly, until mixture thickens and lightly coats back of wooden spoon.

3. Cool custard to room temperature. Stir in vanilla extract. Pour into 3-cup serving dish. Chill until completely set, about 2 hours. Sprinkle surface with chocolate sprinkles.

Makes 4 servings. Each serving has 159 calories.

Faintly Chocolate Parfait

3 tablespoons carob powder or cocoa powder
3 tablespoons strong hot coffee
4 eggs, separated
¼ cup sugar
1 teaspoon vanilla extract
3 cups Low-Calorie Whipped Topping (see page 93)

1. Stir carob or cocoa powder into hot coffee to dissolve. Let mixture cool.

2. Using electric mixer at high speed, beat egg yolks in large bowl until thick and lemon colored. Gradually beat in sugar, keeping mixture smooth. Stir in mocha mixture and vanilla extract.

3. Using electric mixer at high speed, beat egg whites in second large bowl until stiff peaks form. Using rubber spatula, gently fold egg whites into mocha mixture.

4. Using rubber spatula, gently fold in whipped topping. Spoon mixture into 1½-quart mold or soufflé dish. Chill for at least 2 hours to set.

Makes 8 servings. Each serving has 115 calories.

Pots de Crème au Chocolat

⅓ cup sugar

¼ cup semisweet chocolate morsels

2 cups skim milk

3 egg yolks, beaten

½ teaspoon vanilla extract

1 cup Low-Calorie Whipped Topping (see page 93)

1. In small saucepan, combine sugar, chocolate morsels and skim milk. Heat over very low heat, stirring constantly, just until chocolate is dissolved.

2. Beat egg yolks in medium bowl; slowly beat in hot milk mixture. Return mixture to saucepan and cook, stirring constantly, until mixture is thickened and lightly coats back of wooden spoon.

3. Cool slightly; stir in vanilla extract and chill until semi-set, at least 1 hour. Using rubber spatula, gently fold in whipped topping to achieve marbled effect.

4. Spoon into four 6-ounce custard cups or chocolate pots. Chill until serving time.

Makes 4 servings. Each serving has 233 calories.

◯ *CalorieSaving Tip:* Pots de crème are a true luxury—once-in-a-while treats for those days when you feel you deserve a little splurge. To lower the calorie count, cut the quantity of sugar and chocolate in half—a thinner pot de crème for a thinner you. Special note on making all calorie-saving custards: always use a wooden spoon to stir the hot liquid (the handle doesn't get hot) and to help you judge whether the custard is thickening properly—the custard should coat the back of the spoon to give a slightly blue color. Cook custards either over or in hot water. Top-of-stove custards should be stirred in the top of a double boiler over hot (not boiling) water. Baked custards should be placed in a baking dish to which hot water is added; the water should come about two-thirds of the way up the custard cups.

Just Chocolate Tortoni

2 eggs, separated
¼ cup sugar
¼ cup skim milk
2 cups Low-Calorie Whipped Topping (see page 93)
1 teaspoon vanilla extract
½ teaspoon almond extract
¼ cup chopped blanched almonds
2 tablespoons chocolate sprinkles

1. Using electric mixer at high speed, beat egg yolks in medium bowl until thick and lemon colored. Gradually beat in sugar, keeping mixture smooth.

2. Heat skim milk to boiling point in small saucepan over medium heat. Using electric mixer at high speed, beat hot milk and vanilla and almond extracts into egg mixture. Using rubber spatula, fold in whipped topping. Freeze until just set, about 3 hours.

3. Using electric mixer at high speed, beat egg whites in medium bowl until stiff. Using mixer at high speed, beat frozen egg yolk mixture until smooth. Using rubber spatula, fold in beaten egg whites, almonds and chocolate sprinkles. Spoon into sixteen 2-ounce paper cups or tortoni cups; freeze for 2 hours.

Makes 16 servings. Each serving has 54 calories.

Note: Serve one dessert to each person; cover remaining desserts with plastic wrap and store in freezer.

Chocolate Tapioca Desserts

⅓ cup quick-cooking tapioca
¼ cup sugar
¼ cup carob powder or cocoa powder
4 cups skim milk
2 eggs, beaten
1 teaspoon vanilla extract
¼ teaspoon almond extract

1. In medium saucepan, blend tapioca, sugar, carob or cocoa powder and milk. Bring to boiling point over medium heat, stirring constantly until thickened.

2. Remove from heat. Rapidly beat in beaten eggs and vanilla and almond extracts. Divide mixture among four 10-ounce custard cups or individual serving dishes. Cool and chill.

Makes 4 servings. Each serving has 230 calories.

Chocolate-Pineapple Whip

two 8-ounce containers lowfat
  pineapple-flavored yogurt
2 tablespoons carob powder
  or cocoa powder
⅛ teaspoon mint extract
2 egg whites
1 tablespoon sugar

1. In medium bowl, combine yogurt, carob or cocoa powder and mint extract, stirring to blend well.

2. Using electric mixer at high speed, beat egg whites in another medium bowl until soft peaks form. Slowly add sugar, beating until egg whites are stiff.

3. Using rubber spatula, fold egg whites into yogurt mixture. Divide among 4 large parfait glasses. Chill for 1 hour; serve immediately—this dessert does not keep.

Makes 4 servings. Each serving has 69 calories.

Baked Chocolate Custard

one 1-ounce square
  unsweetened chocolate
2 cups skim milk
½ cup sugar
¼ cup flour
2 tablespoons diet margarine,
  melted
3 eggs, separated
1 teaspoon vanilla extract

1. Preheat oven to 325° F.

2. Melt chocolate in top of double boiler over hot (not boiling) water. Slowly stir in skim milk; add sugar. Stir to blend and to dissolve sugar. Remove from heat.

3. In medium bowl, blend flour, melted diet margarine and egg yolks, stirring until smooth. Stir in vanilla extract. Add to milk mixture; beat until smooth.

4. Using electric mixer at high speed, beat egg whites in medium bowl until stiff. Using rubber spatula, fold into milk mixture. Pour into 1-quart casserole with nonstick finish.

5. Place casserole in shallow roasting pan and add hot water to pan to depth of 1 inch. Bake for 50 to 60 minutes, until knife inserted in center comes out clean.

Makes 8 servings. Each serving has 136 calories.

Baked Chocolate Provençal

1 cup evaporated skim milk

½ cup sugar

⅓ cup carob powder or cocoa powder

1 tablespoon diet margarine

3 eggs, separated

1 cup fresh bread crumbs

½ cup Low-Calorie Whipped Topping (optional; see page 93)

1. Preheat oven to 350° F.

2. In medium saucepan, combine evaporated milk, sugar, carob or cocoa powder and diet margarine. Heat over low heat, stirring constantly, until sugar is dissolved.

3. Beat egg yolks in small bowl; beat yolks into hot milk mixture. Stir in bread crumbs. Cool completely.

4. Using electric mixer at high speed, beat egg whites in large bowl until very stiff. Using rubber spatula, gently fold egg whites into bread crumb mixture.

5. Spoon into 1½-quart baking dish with nonstick finish. Bake for 40 to 45 minutes. Serve with whipped topping if desired.

Makes 8 servings. Each serving has 141 calories; with topping each serving has 150 calories.

Chocolate Cake

1¾ cups all-purpose flour

2 teaspoons baking powder

¼ teaspoon salt

⅔ cup cocoa

½ cup sugar

½ cup granulated sugar replacement

½ cup diet margarine

½ cup skim milk

½ teaspoon vanilla extract

3 egg whites

1. Preheat oven to 375° F. Use 8-inch round cake pan with nonstick finish if possible; otherwise, lightly grease and flour 8-inch round cake pan.

2. Sift together flour, baking powder and salt; set aside.

3. In large bowl, blend together cocoa, sugar and sugar replacement. Add diet margarine; using electric mixer at low speed, beat to blend well. Stir in half of flour mixture, ¼ cup of the skim milk and the vanilla extract. Stir in remaining flour mixture and skim milk.

4. Using electric mixer at high speed, beat egg whites in medium bowl until stiff peaks form. Using rubber spatula, gently fold into chocolate mixture.

5. Pour batter into prepared pan; bake for 25 minutes or until cake tester inserted in center of cake comes out clean. Remove cake from pan to wire rack to cool completely.

Makes 12 servings. Each serving has 153 calories.

Chocolate Roll

⅔ cup sifted cake flour

⅓ cup carob powder or cocoa powder

¾ teaspoon baking powder

6 eggs

½ cup sugar

1 teaspoon vanilla extract

2 cups Low-Calorie Whipped Topping (see page 93)

1. Preheat oven to 350° F. Line 15 x 9 x 1-inch jelly roll pan with waxed paper; grease lightly.

2. Sift cake flour again along with carob or cocoa powder and baking powder. Set aside.

3. Using electric mixer at high speed, beat eggs in large bowl until thick and lemon colored. Gradually beat in sugar, keeping mixture smooth. Stir in vanilla extract.

4. Using rubber spatula, fold one-third of flour mixture at a time into beaten eggs. Spoon batter into prepared pan.

5. Bake for 15 to 18 minutes or until surface springs back when lightly touched with finger. Invert cake onto clean dish towel; quickly strip off paper and trim edges of cake with serrated knife.

6. Working from one long edge, roll up jelly-roll fashion so cake is wrapped in towel. Place on wire rack to cool. Unroll cake and remove towel; spread whipped topping over cake and roll up again.

Makes 12 servings. Each serving has 122 calories.

Chocolate-Mint Angel Cake

one 16-ounce package angel
food cake mix

2 cups Low-Calorie Whipped
Topping (see page 93)

½ cup carob powder or
cocoa powder

2 tablespoons sugar

½ teaspoon peppermint
extract

1. Prepare angel food cake according to label directions. Cool cake completely; cut horizontally into 3 layers.

2. One hour before serving, prepare filling by gently combining whipped topping, carob or cocoa powder, sugar and peppermint extract in medium bowl with rubber spatula.

3. Place bottom layer of cake on serving platter; cover with ⅔ cup filling. Set second layer in place; spread another ⅔ cup filling on top. Set third layer in place and frost top with remaining filling. Chill cake for 1 hour.

Makes 12 servings. Each serving has 172 calories.

Note: This cake stores well in refrigerator or freezer.

Chocolate Chip Cookies

½ cup diet margarine

¼ cup granulated sugar
replacement

¼ cup brown sugar, firmly
packed

¼ teaspoon vanilla extract

1 cup sifted all-purpose flour

¼ teaspoon baking powder

⅛ teaspoon salt

¼ cup semisweet chocolate
morsels

1. Preheat oven to 375° F.

2. Using electric mixer at high speed, beat together diet margarine, sugar replacement and brown sugar in medium bowl until creamy; beat in vanilla extract. With mixer at low speed, stir in sifted flour, baking powder and salt; blend thoroughly. Stir in chocolate morsels.

3. Drop by rounded teaspoonfuls 2 inches apart onto cookie sheet with nonstick finish. Bake for 10 to 12 minutes. Cool on cookie sheet for 2 minutes, then remove cookies to wire rack to cool completely.

Makes 22 cookies. Each cookie has 60 calories.

Hot Chocolate Alexander

4 cups skim milk
2 tablespoons instant freeze-dried coffee
2 tablespoons chocolate syrup
½ teaspoon vanilla extract
½ teaspoon brandy extract
½ cup Low-Calorie Whipped Topping (see page 93)

1. Heat skim milk, instant coffee and chocolate syrup in medium saucepan over medium heat until piping hot, stirring to dissolve coffee.

2. Remove from heat. Stir in vanilla and brandy extracts. Divide mixture among four 10-ounce heatproof glasses. Top each with 2 tablespoons whipped topping. Serve immediately.

Makes 4 servings. Each serving has 177 calories. Shown on page 68.

Chocolate Minarets

½ cup water
¼ cup diet margarine
½ cup sifted flour
2 eggs

FILLING

3 tablespoons evaporated skim milk
3 tablespoons carob powder or cocoa powder
½ cup lowfat cottage cheese
2 tablespoons sugar
1 teaspoon vanilla extract

1. Preheat oven to 400° F.

2. Bring water and diet margarine to boiling point in small saucepan over medium heat, stirring to melt margarine. Add sifted flour all at once. Beat until mixture leaves sides of pan; heat 30 seconds longer. Remove from heat; add eggs one at a time, beating thoroughly after each addition.

3. On baking sheet with nonstick finish, make 4 mounds of 2 tablespoons mixture each; make 4 small mounds of 1 teaspoon mixture each. Bake puffs for 20 minutes; remove small puffs to wire rack to cool. Bake large puffs 20 minutes longer; remove to rack to cool.

4. Meanwhile, make filling by heating evaporated milk and carob or cocoa powder in small saucepan; stir until powder is dissolved. Remove from heat; stir in cottage cheese, sugar and vanilla extract. Cool and chill.

5. Cut ½-inch slice off tops of large puffs. Fill each large puff with filling. Place small puffs on top of filling to form minaret.

Makes 4 servings. Each serving has 186 calories.

Norwegian Omelets

4 slices pound cake, ¼ inch thick
1 pint chocolate ice milk
2 egg whites
⅛ teaspoon cream of tartar
⅛ teaspoon salt
1 tablespoon sugar

1. Place pound cake slices on foil-lined cookie sheet. Using metal spatula, quickly shape ½ cup ice milk to fit top of each slice. Freeze until very firm, at least 1 hour.

2. Preheat oven to 500° F.

3. Using electric mixer at high speed, beat egg whites, cream of tartar and salt in medium bowl until soft peaks form. Sprinkle in sugar; beat until egg whites are stiff.

4. Swirl meringue evenly over each portion of cake and ice milk to cover completely. Bake for 3 to 5 minutes or until lightly browned. Serve immediately.

Makes 4 servings. Each serving has 177 calories.

Pears in Honey-Chocolate Sauce

one 29-ounce can pear halves
½ cup water
¼ cup honey
one 1-ounce square unsweetened chocolate
½ teaspoon vanilla extract

1. Drain pear halves very well. Place 2 pear halves in each of 4 dessert glasses. Chill until serving time.

2. Just before serving, blend water and honey in small saucepan over low heat; stir well. Add chocolate; stir constantly until chocolate is melted and sauce is syrupy. Remove from heat; stir in vanilla extract.

3. Spoon 1 tablespoon chocolate sauce over each serving of pears. (Pour the rest into a screw-top jar and refrigerate for later use.)

Makes 4 servings. Each serving has 179 calories.

Black Bottom Pie

¼ cup vanilla wafer crumbs
1 envelope unflavored gelatin
¼ cup water
½ cup sugar
¼ cup flour
2 cups skim milk
3 eggs, separated
⅓ cup carob powder or cocoa powder
1½ teaspoons vanilla extract

1. Spread vanilla wafer crumbs over bottom of 9-inch pie plate. Set aside.

2. Sprinkle gelatin over water in small custard cup; let soften for 5 minutes.

3. In top of double boiler, blend ⅓ cup of the sugar, the flour and ½ cup of the skim milk. Beat in egg yolks. Heat remaining skim milk to boiling point in small saucepan over low heat; slowly beat into egg mixture.

4. Place top of double boiler over boiling water, taking care that bottom of pan does not touch water. Cook, stirring constantly, until mixture lightly coats back of wooden spoon.

5. Remove from heat; stir in softened gelatin to dissolve. Remove 1 cup custard from pan and set aside to cool. Add carob or cocoa powder and 1 teaspoon of the vanilla extract to custard remaining in pan; cool, then chill until it is consistency of unbeaten egg whites, 30 to 45 minutes. Pour into prepared pie plate; chill until completely set, 30 to 45 minutes.

6. Using electric mixer at high speed, beat egg whites in large bowl until soft peaks form; slowly add remaining sugar, beating until egg whites are stiff. Using rubber spatula, fold in reserved custard and remaining ½ teaspoon vanilla extract; mound on custard in pie plate. Chill for 2 hours.

Makes 8 servings. Each serving has 161 calories.

⊙ *CalorieSaving Tip:* Because carob powder has a milder flavor than cocoa, it requires less sweetening. If you decide to use carob powder instead of cocoa in the recipe above, ⅓ cup sugar is all the sweetener you'll need for optimum flavor. Add ¼ cup of the sugar to the custard mixture, and the remainder to the beaten egg whites.

Blanche et Noire Tarte

1 envelope unflavored gelatin
1¾ cups skim milk
2 eggs, separated
½ cup sugar
1½ teaspoons vanilla extract
2 tablespoons carob powder
   or cocoa powder
¼ cup vanilla wafer crumbs

1. Sprinkle gelatin over ¼ cup of the skim milk in small custard cup; let stand for 5 minutes to soften.

2. In small saucepan, combine remaining milk, the egg yolks and sugar. Heat over low heat, stirring constantly, until mixture thickens and lightly coats back of wooden spoon. Stir in softened gelatin to dissolve.

3. Divide mixture in half. Stir carob or cocoa powder into one half to dissolve. Beat egg whites in small bowl until stiff; using rubber spatula, fold into second half. Chill both mixtures until semi-set, about 1 hour.

4. Press vanilla wafer crumbs over bottom and sides of lightly greased 8-inch pie plate. Spread chocolate filling over bottom; top with plain filling. Chill 1 hour longer.

Makes 8 servings. Each serving has 107 calories.

Chocolate Cheese Pie

¼ cup graham cracker
   crumbs
1 teaspoon sugar
1 cup lowfat cottage cheese
½ cup brown sugar, lightly
   packed
⅓ cup carob powder or
   cocoa powder
¼ cup evaporated skim milk
2 eggs, separated
1 teaspoon vanilla extract
2 cups Low-Calorie Whipped
   Topping (see page 93)

1. Combine graham cracker crumbs and sugar. Spread over bottom of 9-inch pie plate. Set aside.

2 Using electric mixer at medium speed, beat together cheese, brown sugar, carob or cocoa powder, evaporated milk, egg yolks and vanilla extract in medium bowl until very smooth.

3. Using electric mixer at high speed, beat egg whites in small bowl until stiff. Using rubber spatula, fold egg whites into cheese mixture, then fold in whipped topping. Spoon filling into pie plate. Chill for 12 hours or overnight.

Makes 8 servings. Each serving has 125 calories.

Chocolate-Mint Chiffon Pie

¼ cup vanilla wafer crumbs

1 teaspoon carob powder or cocoa powder

1 envelope unflavored gelatin

¼ cup carob or cocoa powder

¼ cup sugar

½ cup skim milk

3 eggs, separated

½ teaspoon peppermint extract

2 cups Low-Calorie Whipped Topping (see page 93)

1. Combine vanilla wafer crumbs and 1 teaspoon carob or cocoa powder. Spread over bottom of 9-inch pie plate. Set crust aside.

2. In medium saucepan, combine gelatin, ¼ cup carob or cocoa powder and 2 tablespoons of the sugar. Stir in skim milk and egg yolks; beat well.

3. Heat over very low heat, stirring constantly to dissolve gelatin. Remove from heat and stir in peppermint extract; cool, and chill until mixture is consistency of unbeaten egg whites, about 1 hour.

4. Using electric mixer at high speed, beat egg whites in medium bowl until soft peaks form. Slowly add remaining 2 tablespoons sugar, beating until egg whites are stiff.

5. Using rubber spatula, carefully fold beaten egg whites and whipped topping into gelatin mixture. Spoon mixture into prepared pie plate. Chill for 12 hours or overnight.

Makes 8 servings. Each serving has 116 calories. Shown on page 69.

⊘ *CalorieSaving Tip:* Choose from a variety of crackers and cookies to make tasty crumb piecrusts that won't spoil your diet. The lowest-calorie crackers to use in crust are zwieback and graham crackers; however, you might want to make them more appealing with a touch of sugar and flavoring—try spicing them up with a little ground cinnamon or grated nutmeg. You can also use the crushed crumbs of presweetened cookies like vanilla wafers or gingersnaps. Try to keep the calorie count to a minimum by spreading the crumbs very thinly over the bottom of a lightly greased pie plate.

Chocolate-Chestnut Soufflé

2 tablespoons diet margarine
2 tablespoons flour
1 cup skim milk
1 cup unsweetened chestnut puree
⅓ cup sugar
⅓ cup carob powder or cocoa powder
4 eggs, separated
½ teaspoon vanilla extract
½ teaspoon brandy extract

1. Preheat oven to 375° F.

2. Melt diet margarine in medium saucepan over low heat; blend in flour. Remove from heat. Beat in skim milk, chestnut puree, sugar and carob or cocoa powder until smooth.

3. Return to heat and cook, stirring constantly, until mixture comes to boiling point. Remove from heat; set aside.

4. Using electric mixer at high speed, beat egg yolks in large bowl until thick and lemon colored. Gradually beat in hot milk mixture. Cool completely.

5. Using electric mixer at high speed, beat egg whites in another large bowl until stiff. Using rubber spatula, gently fold into chocolate-chestnut mixture. Fold in vanilla and brandy extracts.

6. Spoon into 1½-quart soufflé dish with nonstick finish. Pour boiling water into roasting pan to depth of ¾ inch; place soufflé dish in roasting pan. Bake for 40 to 50 minutes or until soufflé is puffed and set on top.

Makes 8 servings. Each serving has 158 calories.

Note: Unsweetened chestnut puree can be found in supermarket gourmet sections, especially during the winter holiday season, and in specialty food shops. To make your own, shell fresh chestnuts, then cook and skin them. Rub the chestnuts through a fine sieve or puree them in a food processor.

Chilled and Frozen Desserts

Chilled and frozen desserts always seem so festive, partly because they're prepared ahead — by the time they're ready to serve, you're cool, relaxed and enjoying your role as easy-going host or hostess.

Dieting's a breeze with cold sweets like Strawberry Custard, totaling only 98 calories a serving, and — believe it or not — a No-Bake Cheesecake at 147 calories a slice. What could be more refreshing on a warm summer day than a tangy Lemon Parfait spooned up in tall glasses, or a frothy Orange-Lemon Mousse served in fresh orange shells?

Gelatin is the only ingredient to watch here. It's important to follow directions for softening, which vary depending on the recipe. Usually gelatin and sugar can be blended with a large amount of liquid without preliminary softening. But if softened and heated directly in milk, the gelatin will cause curdling. Never freeze food containing gelatin unless it's specified in the recipe, since the dish can turn to liquid.

Whether molded or spooned into individual dishes, cold desserts lend themselves particularly well to attractive garnishes — a whole strawberry here, a sprig of fresh mint there. Appearances are especially important when you're dieting. A beautifully presented smaller portion can be more satisfying than a carelessly served larger helping.

Looking for a cool, refreshing sweet? Your search is over.

Low-Calorie Whipped Topping

1 envelope unflavored gelatin
1¼ cups ice water
1 cup nonfat dry milk powder
¼ cup lowfat unflavored yogurt
1 tablespoon lemon juice
1 teaspoon grated lemon rind

1. Sprinkle gelatin over ¼ cup of the ice water in small saucepan; let stand for 5 minutes to soften. Place over very low heat just until gelatin is dissolved; cool.

2. Meanwhile, sprinkle dry milk powder over remaining 1 cup water in medium bowl; chill for 5 minutes in refrigerator.

3. Using electric mixer at high speed, beat dry milk mixture until soft peaks form. Gradually beat in cooled gelatin, yogurt, lemon juice and lemon rind.

4. Use in recipes specifying Low-Calorie Whipped Topping or to swirl over fruit salads and other low-calorie desserts.

Makes 3 cups. Each cup has 153 calories.

Note: Covered with plastic wrap, this topping will store up to 2 hours in the refrigerator. It must be rebeaten before it is used.

Almond Cream

1 envelope unflavored gelatin
1¾ cups skim milk
2 tablespoons sugar
½ teaspoon almond extract
2 egg whites
1 cup sliced fresh strawberries

1. Sprinkle gelatin over ¼ cup of the skim milk in small bowl; let stand for 5 minutes to soften.

2. Bring remaining skim milk and the sugar to boiling point in medium saucepan over medium heat. Remove from heat; add softened gelatin and stir to dissolve. Add almond extract. Cool, then chill until semi-set, 30 to 45 minutes.

3. Using electric mixer at high speed, beat egg whites in medium bowl until stiff peaks form. Using mixer at high speed, beat gelatin mixture until foamy.

4. Using rubber spatula, fold egg whites into gelatin mixture. Divide among 4 dessert dishes. Top with sliced strawberries.

Makes 4 servings. Each serving has 90 calories.

Apple Meringue

2 egg whites
⅛ teaspoon cream of tartar
⅛ teaspoon salt
1 tablespoon sugar
1 cup unsweetened applesauce
1 teaspoon grated lemon rind

1. Using electric mixer at high speed, beat egg whites, cream of tartar and salt in medium bowl until soft peaks form. Sprinkle in sugar; beat until egg whites are stiff. Using rubber spatula, gently fold in applesauce and lemon rind.

2. Pour carefully into 4 parfait glasses; chill. Serve within 4 to 6 hours—this dessert does not keep.

Makes 4 servings. Each serving has 45 calories.

Banana-Nut Parfaits

1 envelope unflavored gelatin
1 cup skim milk
1 medium banana, thinly sliced
1 tablespoon brown sugar
½ teaspoon vanilla extract
¼ teaspoon nutmeg
1 cup vanilla ice milk
1 tablespoon finely chopped pecans or walnuts

1. Sprinkle gelatin over ½ cup of the skim milk in medium bowl; let stand for 5 minutes to soften.

2. Bring remaining ½ cup skim milk to boiling point in small saucepan; pour into gelatin mixture. Stir to dissolve gelatin; cool slightly.

3. Add banana slices, brown sugar, vanilla extract and nutmeg. Stir in ice milk. Chill until semi-set, 30 to 45 minutes.

4. Spoon banana mixture into 4 parfait glasses; chill until completely set, about 1½ hours. Sprinkle top of each with ¾ teaspoon chopped nuts.

Makes 4 servings. Each serving has 126 calories.

   CalorieSaving Tip: Nuts can be a real dessert treat—but because their fat content is so high, they can also undermine your careful calorie counting. If you have the patience to shell them, choose pistachios—they have the fewest calories. Avoid Brazil nuts—they're at the highest end of the calorie spectrum.

Bavarian Cheese Cream

1 envelope unflavored gelatin
¾ cup skim milk
2 eggs, separated
¼ cup sugar
1 cup lowfat, small curd cottage cheese
1 tablespoon lemon juice
½ teaspoon vanilla extract
½ cup frozen whipped topping

1. Sprinkle gelatin over ¼ cup of the skim milk in small bowl; let stand for 5 minutes to soften.

2. In top of double boiler, beat egg yolks, sugar and remaining skim milk. Cook over simmering water, stirring constantly, until mixture thickens and lightly coats back of wooden spoon. Add softened gelatin and stir to dissolve. Remove from heat; stir in cottage cheese, lemon juice and vanilla extract.

3. Using electric mixer at high speed, beat egg whites in small bowl until stiff. Using rubber spatula, fold into cheese mixture along with whipped topping. Divide mixture among four 10-ounce custard cups; chill until completely set, about 1 hour.

Makes 4 servings. Each serving has 219 calories.

Cherry Foam

one 3-ounce package cherry-flavored gelatin
1 cup boiling water
¾ cup ice water
1 tablespoon lemon juice
1 teaspoon grated lemon rind
2 egg whites

TOPPING

¾ cup nonfat dry milk powder
¼ cup ice water

1. In medium bowl, blend gelatin and boiling water; stir to dissolve gelatin. Blend in ¾ cup ice water, lemon juice and lemon rind. Chill until semi-set, about 1 hour.

2. Using electric mixer at high speed, beat egg whites in large bowl until stiff peaks form. Using mixer at high speed, beat gelatin mixture in another bowl until light and fluffy.

3. Using rubber spatula, fold gelatin mixture into egg whites. Spoon into four 10-ounce custard cups; chill until completely set, at least 2 hours.

4. To make topping, blend dry milk powder and ¼ cup ice water in small bowl; using electric mixer at high speed, beat until stiff.

5. To serve, unmold each dessert onto individual plate. Top each with 1 tablespoon topping.

Makes 4 servings. Each serving has 108 calories.

Coffee Parfaits

2 cups skim milk
⅓ cup brown sugar, lightly packed
2 tablespoons instant coffee
4 eggs, separated
2 cups Low-Calorie Whipped Topping (see page 93)

1. In medium saucepan, combine skim milk, brown sugar and instant coffee; heat over low heat until bubbles form at edge.

2. Beat egg yolks in medium bowl; gradually beat in hot coffee mixture. Return mixture to saucepan and cook over low heat, stirring constantly, until mixture lightly coats back of wooden spoon. Cool, then chill mixture until semi-set, at least 1 hour.

3. Using electric mixer at high speed, beat egg whites until stiff. Using rubber spatula, fold into coffee mixture.

4. To make parfaits, alternate layers of coffee mixture and whipped topping in 8 parfait glasses.

Makes 8 servings. Each serving has 113 calories.

Note: Extra Coffee Parfaits store well for up to 2 days. Cover tops loosely with plastic wrap.

Cranberry Whip

1 envelope unflavored gelatin
¼ cup sugar
1¾ cups cranberry juice cocktail
½ teaspoon grated orange rind

1. Combine gelatin, sugar and ½ cup of the cranberry juice in small saucepan; place over very low heat just until gelatin is dissolved.

2. Stir in remaining cranberry juice and the orange rind. Place in large bowl. Chill until mixture is consistency of unbeaten egg whites, 30 to 45 minutes.

3. Using electric mixer at high speed, beat cranberry mixture until light and fluffy. Divide among 4 dessert dishes; chill until set, about 1 hour.

Makes 4 servings. Each serving has 127 calories.

Creamy Charlotte

8 ladyfingers, split
1 envelope unflavored gelatin
¾ cup skim milk
¼ cup confectioners' sugar
1 teaspoon brandy extract or vanilla extract
1 cup evaporated skim milk, chilled

1. Line 4-cup mold with ladyfingers, placing cut side toward center. Set aside.

2. Sprinkle gelatin over ¼ cup of the skim milk in small saucepan; let stand for 5 minutes to soften. Place over very low heat just until gelatin is dissolved.

3. Stir in remaining skim milk, the confectioners' sugar and brandy or vanilla extract. Chill until semi-set, about 30 minutes.

4. Using electric mixer at high speed, beat evaporated milk in medium bowl until it is consistency of whipped topping. Using rubber spatula, fold into gelatin mixture. Spoon into mold lined with ladyfingers; chill for 1 hour.

Makes 8 servings. Each serving has 83 calories.

Lemon Parfaits

1 envelope unflavored gelatin
¼ cup cold water
2 eggs, beaten
one 6-ounce can lemonade concentrate
one 13-ounce can evaporated skim milk, chilled

1. Sprinkle gelatin over cold water in small saucepan; let stand for 5 minutes to soften. Place over very low heat just until gelatin is dissolved.

2. Blend in beaten eggs; heat for 1 minute longer, stirring constantly until eggs are slightly thickened. Remove from heat; stir in lemonade concentrate. Chill until mixture is semi-set, about 30 minutes.

3. Using electric mixer at high speed, beat evaporated milk in large bowl until it is consistency of whipped cream. Using rubber spatula, fold into gelatin mixture.

4. Divide lemon mixture among 4 large parfait glasses. Chill for at least 1 hour.

Makes 4 servings. Each serving has 116 calories.

Lime Mousse

1 envelope unflavored gelatin
¼ cup skim milk
½ cup boiling water
1 cup lime sherbet
one 13-ounce can evaporated
  skim milk, chilled

1. Sprinkle gelatin over ¼ cup skim milk in small bowl; let stand for 5 minutes to soften. Add boiling water; stir until gelatin is completely dissolved. Stir in lime sherbet; cool slightly.

2. Using electric mixer at high speed, beat evaporated milk in medium bowl until it is consistency of whipped cream. Using rubber spatula, fold into lime sherbet mixture.

3. Divide mixture among 4 individual soufflé dishes or 10-ounce custard cups; chill until completely set, about 1 hour.

Makes 4 servings. Each serving has 215 calories.

Orange-Lemon Mousse

4 large oranges, hollowed out
1 envelope unflavored gelatin
2 tablespoons sugar
⅓ cup orange juice
⅓ cup lemon juice
1 tablespoon grated lemon
  rind
4 eggs, separated

1. Cut ½-inch slice from top of each orange; using teaspoon, scoop out orange pulp. Set orange shells aside. Press pulp through strainer to yield ⅓ cup juice.

2. In small saucepan, combine gelatin, sugar, orange juice, lemon juice and lemon rind. Place over very low heat just until gelatin is dissolved.

3. Using electric mixer at high speed, beat egg yolks in large bowl until thick and lemon colored. Slowly beat in orange-lemon mixture. Pour into large bowl. Chill until semi-set, 30 to 45 minutes; beat until fluffy.

4. In another large bowl, beat egg whites until stiff. Using rubber spatula, fold into orange-lemon mixture. Spoon into orange shells; chill until completely set, about 1 hour.

Makes 4 servings. Each serving has 144 calories. Shown on page 70.

Orange Snow

1 envelope unflavored gelatin
1½ cups orange juice
1 teaspoon grated orange rind
2 egg whites

1. Sprinkle gelatin over ½ cup of the orange juice in small saucepan; let stand for 5 minutes to soften. Place over very low heat just until gelatin is dissolved.

2. Stir in remaining orange juice and the orange rind; chill until semi-set, about 1 hour.

3. Using electric mixer at high speed, beat egg whites in medium bowl until stiff peaks form. Using rubber spatula, gently fold into semi-set orange mixture.

4. Spoon into 3-cup mold; chill until completely set, about 1 hour. Dip mold quickly into hot water and invert onto serving platter; shake to release mold.

Makes 4 servings. Each serving has 56 calories.

Peanutty Perfections

1 envelope unflavored gelatin
1 tablespoon sugar
1 cup skim milk
1 teaspoon vanilla extract
1 cup vanilla ice milk
1 medium banana, peeled and thinly sliced
¼ cup chopped peanuts

1. In small saucepan, blend gelatin, sugar and milk. Place over very low heat just until gelatin is dissolved. Cool slightly; stir in vanilla extract. Pour into medium bowl.

2. Chill until mixture is consistency of unbeaten egg whites, about 30 minutes. Add ice milk; using electric mixer at high speed, beat until foamy.

3. Alternate layers of vanilla mixture, bananas and peanuts in 4 large parfait glasses. Chill 1 hour longer.

Makes 4 servings. Each serving has 166 calories.

Pineapple Squares

1 cup graham cracker crumbs

2 tablespoons diet margarine, melted

1 envelope unflavored gelatin

¼ cup skim milk

3 eggs, separated

one 8-ounce can crushed pineapple in natural juices

2 tablespoons sugar

2 tablespoons lemon juice

1 teaspoon grated lemon rind

1 cup lowfat, small curd cottage cheese

1. Blend together graham cracker crumbs and melted diet margarine. Pat over bottom of 8 x 8 x 2-inch baking pan; chill.

2. Sprinkle gelatin over skim milk in small bowl; let stand for 5 minutes to soften.

3. Using electric mixer at medium speed, beat egg yolks in top of double boiler until lemon colored. Add undrained crushed pineapple, sugar, lemon juice and lemon rind. Cook over simmering water until thickened, stirring constantly. Stir in softened gelatin to dissolve; stir in cottage cheese and chill until semi-set, about 1 hour.

4. Using electric mixer at high speed, beat egg whites in large bowl until stiff peaks form. Using rubber spatula, fold into gelatin mixture. Pour into prepared pan. Chill until completely set, about 1 hour. To serve, cut into 2-inch squares.

Makes 16 squares. Each square has 61 calories.

Sherry Cream Mold

1 envelope unflavored gelatin

¾ cup skim milk

¼ cup sugar

2 eggs, separated

¼ cup dry sherry

1½ cups Low-Calorie Whipped Topping (see page 93)

1. Sprinkle gelatin over skim milk in top of double boiler; let stand for 5 minutes to soften. Place over boiling water, taking care that pan does not touch water. Stir to dissolve gelatin.

2. Add sugar and egg yolks; stir constantly until mixture thickens and lightly coats back of wooden spoon. Stir in sherry. Chill until semi-set, 30 to 45 minutes.

3. Using electric mixer at high speed, beat egg whites in medium bowl until very stiff. Using rubber spatula, fold egg whites and whipped topping into sherry mixture.

4. Spoon mixture into 1-quart mold. Chill until completely set, at least 2 hours. Dip mold into hot water and invert onto serving platter; shake to release mold. Chill 5 minutes longer.

Makes 4 servings. Each serving has 170 calories.

Strawberry Custard

2 eggs, separated
¼ cup sugar
1 cup skim milk
1 envelope unflavored gelatin
½ teaspoon vanilla extract
½ teaspoon almond extract
2 cups sliced fresh strawberries
2 cups Low-Calorie Whipped Topping (see page 93)

1. In small saucepan, combine egg yolks, sugar and ¾ cup of the skim milk. Heat over low heat, stirring constantly, until sugar is dissolved and mixture is thickened and lightly coats back of wooden spoon.

2. Meanwhile, sprinkle gelatin over remaining ¼ cup skim milk in small custard cup; let stand for 5 minutes to soften. Stir into egg yolk mixture to dissolve gelatin. Pour into large bowl and cool.

3. Stir in vanilla and almond extracts. Gently stir in sliced strawberries. Chill until syrupy, about 30 minutes.

4. Using electric mixer at high speed, beat egg whites until stiff. Using rubber spatula, fold egg whites and whipped topping into strawberry mixture.

5. Spoon mixture into 1½-quart dessert bowl. Chill until completely set, at least 2 hours.

Makes 8 servings. Each serving has 98 calories.

Strawberry Yogurt Custard

one 16-ounce container lowfat unflavored yogurt
1 cup sliced fresh strawberries
2 tablespoons honey
½ teaspoon almond extract
½ teaspoon vanilla extract
1 cup Low-Calorie Whipped Topping (see page 93)
¼ cup vanilla wafer crumbs

1. In large bowl, blend yogurt, strawberries, honey, and almond and vanilla extracts. Using rubber spatula, gently fold in whipped topping.

2. Divide among 4 parfait glasses and chill until serving time. Sprinkle top of each with 1 tablespoon vanilla wafer crumbs.

Makes 4 servings. Each serving has 165 calories.

Tom and Jerry Desserts

1 envelope unflavored gelatin
¼ cup sugar
3 eggs, separated
1¼ cups skim milk
1 teaspoon rum extract
½ teaspoon brandy extract
¼ teaspoon nutmeg

1. In medium saucepan, blend gelatin, 2 tablespoons of the sugar and the egg yolks. Gradually stir in skim milk; let stand for 5 minutes to soften gelatin.

2. Cook over low heat, stirring constantly, until gelatin is dissolved. Cool slightly; add rum and brandy extracts. Chill until semi-set, about 1 hour.

3. Meanwhile, use electric mixer at high speed to beat egg whites in large bowl until soft peaks form. Sprinkle in remaining 2 tablespoons sugar, beating until egg whites are stiff.

4. Using rubber spatula, gently fold egg whites into gelatin mixture. Divide among 4 large parfait glasses; chill until completely set, about 1 hour.

Makes 4 servings. Each serving has 140 calories.

Wine Pudding

1½ cups dry white wine
¼ cup water
3 eggs, slightly beaten
¼ cup sugar

1. Heat wine and water in top of double boiler over boiling water until lukewarm.

2. Using wire whisk, beat in slightly beaten eggs and sugar. Beat vigorously until mixture thickens, about 5 to 10 minutes.

3. Remove from heat; continue beating to cool slightly. Pour into 4 dessert dishes; chill for 1 hour.

Makes 4 servings. Each serving has 155 calories.

No-Bake Cheesecake

⅔ cup graham cracker crumbs

2 tablespoons diet margarine, melted

1 envelope unflavored gelatin

one 8-ounce can crushed pineapple in natural juices

½ cup boiling water

one 16-ounce container skim-milk ricotta cheese

⅓ cup granulated sugar replacement

1 teaspoon vanilla extract

1. In small bowl, combine graham cracker crumbs and melted diet margarine with fork. Pat over bottom of 9-inch springform pan; set aside.

2. Drain juice from crushed pineapple into blender container; sprinkle gelatin over juice and let stand for 5 minutes to soften. Add boiling water; blend mixture at high speed until gelatin is dissolved.

3. Add cheese, sugar replacement and vanilla extract. Blend at high speed for 2 minutes, until mixture is smooth.

4. Pour filling over graham cracker crust; chill until set, about 2 to 3 hours. Remove sides of springform pan when ready to cut cheesecake.

Makes 8 servings. Each serving has 147 calories.

Fruited Cheesecake

1 envelope unflavored gelatin

¼ cup sugar

¾ cup skim milk

1 egg, separated

1 tablespoon lemon juice

2 teaspoons grated lemon rind

one 12-ounce container lowfat cottage cheese with fruit salad

¼ cup graham cracker crumbs

⅛ teaspoon cinnamon

1. In small saucepan, blend gelatin and 2 tablespoons of the sugar; stir in ½ cup of the skim milk. Let stand for 5 minutes to soften. Place over very low heat just until gelatin is dissolved.

2. Stir in remaining skim milk, the egg yolk, lemon juice and lemon rind. In medium bowl, beat cottage cheese until smooth. Beat in gelatin mixture; chill until semi-set, about 1 hour.

3. Using electric mixer at high speed, beat egg white in small bowl until soft peaks form; sprinkle in remaining sugar; beat until egg white is stiff. Using rubber spatula, fold into cheese mixture.

4. Spoon mixture into 7- or 8-inch springform pan. Sprinkle top of mixture with graham cracker crumbs and cinnamon. Chill until firm, about 1 hour.

Makes 12 servings. Each serving has 62 calories.

Peach Cheese Pie

1 tablespoon diet margarine

½ cup vanilla wafer crumbs

2 cups lowfat, small curd cottage cheese

½ cup chopped cashews

2 teaspoons vanilla extract

2 cups Low-Calorie Whipped Topping (see page 93)

one 8¾-ounce can cling peach halves, drained

1 cup orange juice

1 tablespoon cornstarch

⅛ teaspoon nutmeg

1. Grease 9-inch pie plate with diet margarine; press vanilla wafer crumbs over bottom and sides of plate to coat. Bake at 400° F for 3 minutes. Set aside to cool.

2. In medium bowl, beat cottage cheese until smooth; stir in cashews and vanilla extract. Using rubber spatula, fold in whipped topping. Spoon mixture into pie plate. Arrange drained cling peach halves on top; chill.

3. In medium saucepan, blend orange juice, cornstarch and nutmeg. Bring to boiling point, stirring constantly. Cool until syrupy; spoon glaze over peaches to coat. Chill pie until served.

Makes 8 servings. Each serving has 176 calories.

Tropical Cream Pie

⅔ cup graham cracker crumbs

2 tablespoons diet margarine, melted

1 envelope unflavored gelatin

½ cup cold water

one 8-ounce can crushed pineapple in natural juices

½ cup apricot nectar

2 tablespoons granulated sugar replacement

¾ cup ice water

½ cup nonfat dry milk powder

2 drops yellow food coloring

1. In small bowl, combine graham cracker crumbs and melted diet margarine with fork. Pat over bottom of 8-inch pie plate; set aside.

2. Sprinkle gelatin over ½ cup cold water in small saucepan; let stand for 5 minutes to soften. Place over low heat just until gelatin is dissolved. In large bowl, combine dissolved gelatin, undrained crushed pineapple, apricot nectar, sugar replacement and ¼ cup of the ice water. Chill until thickened, about 30 minutes.

3. Sprinkle dry milk powder over remaining ½ cup ice water in another large bowl. Using electric mixer at high speed, beat until stiff peaks form.

4. Using mixer at high speed, beat gelatin mixture until foamy. Using rubber spatula, gently fold in dry milk mixture and food coloring. Pour over piecrust; chill until firm, about 1½ hours.

Makes 8 servings. Each serving has 80 calories.

Meringue Pie

3 egg whites
¼ teaspoon cream of tartar
2 tablespoons sugar
1 envelope unflavored gelatin
½ cup cold water
one 10-ounce package frozen raspberries, thawed
¾ cup ice water
½ cup nonfat dry milk powder

1. Preheat oven to 275° F.

2. Using electric mixer at high speed, beat egg whites and cream of tartar in large bowl until foamy. Add sugar, 1 tablespoon at a time; beat at high speed after each addition until egg whites are stiff.

3. Spread meringue over bottom and sides of 9-inch pie plate, forming a high edge. Bake for 40 to 50 minutes, until meringue is lightly browned and dry.

4. Meanwhile, sprinkle gelatin over ½ cup cold water in small saucepan; let stand for 5 minutes to soften. Heat over low heat, stirring constantly, until gelatin is dissolved.

5. Pour gelatin mixture into small bowl; add raspberries and ¼ cup of the ice water. Chill until semi-set, about 30 minutes.

6. Sprinkle dry milk powder over remaining ½ cup ice water in large bowl. Using electric mixer at high speed, beat until stiff peaks form.

7. Using electric mixer at high speed, beat gelatin mixture until foamy. Using rubber spatula, gently fold gelatin mixture in dry milk mixture until well blended. Spoon into meringue shell; chill until firm, about 1 hour.

Makes 8 servings. Each serving has 70 calories.

◎ *CalorieSaving Tip:* Fresh fruit is always preferable to its frozen or canned alter ego, because sugar is generally added to fruit during processing. To reduce the number of calories in processed fruit, drain off all the liquid, and rinse the fruit in cold water if it's been packed in syrup; dry the fruit on paper towels to remove even more syrup. Unfortunately, this results in some loss of flavor as well as calories, so as a rule try to bypass fruit that's been packed in heavy syrup.

Yogurt Ribbon Pie

2 envelopes unflavored gelatin
¼ cup sugar
1 cup skim milk
one 16-ounce container lowfat
  unflavored yogurt
¼ teaspoon peppermint
  extract
2 to 3 drops green food
  coloring
¼ teaspoon almond extract
2 to 3 drops red food coloring
¼ teaspoon vanilla extract
1 teaspoon instant coffee
2 egg whites

1. In small saucepan, combine gelatin, sugar and skim milk. Heat over very low heat, stirring constantly, until gelatin is dissolved. Stir in yogurt.

2. Place ¾ cup mixture in each of 4 small bowls. Add peppermint extract and green food coloring to one bowl; add almond extract and red food coloring to second bowl; add vanilla extract to third bowl; and add instant coffee to fourth bowl. Stir each to blend. Chill all until semi-set, about 30 minutes.

3. Using electric mixer at high speed, beat egg whites in medium bowl until stiff. Using mixer at high speed, beat each gelatin mixture until light and fluffy. Using rubber spatula, fold one-fourth of the beaten egg whites into each of beaten gelatin mixtures.

4. Layer mixtures in 8-inch pie plate, spreading carefully to edge of plate. Chill until completely set, about 30 minutes.

Makes 8 servings. Each serving has 79 calories.

Frozen Apple Strudel Pie

⅔ cup graham cracker
  crumbs
¾ teaspoon cinnamon
2 tablespoons diet margarine,
  melted
1 envelope unflavored gelatin
¼ cup cold water
one 20-ounce can apple slices
1 cup lowfat, unflavored yogurt
⅔ cup nonfat dry milk powder
¼ cup granulated sugar
  replacement

1. In small bowl, combine graham cracker crumbs, ¼ teaspoon of the cinnamon and the melted diet margarine with fork. Pat over bottom of 9-inch springform pan; chill.

2. Sprinkle gelatin over cold water in blender container; let stand for 5 minutes to soften.

3. Drain juice from apple slices into liquid measure; add enough water to measure 1 cup. Pour into small saucepan; heat to boiling point and add to softened gelatin in blender container. Blend at medium speed until gelatin is dissolved.

4. Add apple slices, yogurt, dry milk powder, sugar replacement and remaining ½ teaspoon cinnamon. Blend at high speed until smooth; pour into 8 x 8 x 2-inch metal pan and freeze until semi-set, about 1 hour.

5. Place mixture in large bowl; using electric mixer at high speed, beat until smooth. Pour over piecrust; freeze until firm, about 2 to 3 hours.

6. To cut, thaw briefly at room temperature and remove sides of pan. Immediately return surplus pie to freezer.

Makes 10 servings. Each serving has 110 calories.

Frozen Blueberry-Banana Pie

GRAHAM CRACKER CRUST

⅔ cup graham cracker crumbs

2 tablespoons diet margarine, melted

FILLING

1 envelope unflavored gelatin

¼ cup cold water

1 cup boiling water

1 cup lowfat unflavored yogurt

one 12-ounce package frozen unsweetened blueberries, thawed

1 medium banana, peeled and sliced

⅔ cup nonfat dry milk powder

2 tablespoons granulated sugar replacement

1. In small bowl, combine graham cracker crumbs and melted diet margarine with fork. Pat over bottom of 9-inch springform pan; chill.

2. Sprinkle gelatin over cold water in blender container; let stand for 5 minutes to soften. Add boiling water and blend at medium speed until gelatin is dissolved.

3. Add yogurt, blueberries, banana, dry milk powder and sugar replacement. Blend at high speed until smooth; pour mixture into 8 x 8 x 2-inch metal pan and freeze until semi-set, about 1 hour.

4. Place mixture in large bowl; using electric mixer at high speed, beat until smooth. Pour over piecrust; freeze until firm, about 2 to 3 hours.

5. To cut, thaw briefly at room temperature and remove sides of pan. Immediately return surplus pie to freezer.

Makes 10 servings. Each serving has 103 calories.

Apricot-Pineapple Frost

1½ cups apricot nectar
one 8-ounce can pineapple
   chunks in natural juices
½ cup crushed ice
1 egg white

1. In electric blender, blend all ingredients at high speed until thick and smooth, about 30 to 40 seconds.

2. Pour ¾ cup mixture into each of four 8-ounce serving glasses. Serve immediately, with two thick straws or iced tea spoon in each.

Makes 4 servings. Each serving has 46 calories.

Cappuccino Shake

1 pint vanilla ice milk
½ cup crushed ice
½ cup water
1 teaspoon instant coffee
¼ teaspoon cinnamon

1. In electric blender, blend all ingredients at high speed until thick and smooth, about 30 to 45 seconds.

2. Pour ¾ cup mixture into each of four 8-ounce serving glasses. Serve immediately, with two thick straws or iced tea spoon in each.

Makes 4 servings. Each serving has 104 calories.

Cranberry Milk Ice

2 cups crushed ice
1½ cups cranberry juice
½ cup orange juice
⅓ cup nonfat dry milk powder

1. In electric blender, blend 1 cup of the crushed ice, the cranberry juice, orange juice and dry milk powder at high speed until smooth, about 30 seconds.

2. Add remaining 1 cup crushed ice and blend until thick and smooth, about 30 seconds longer.

3. Pour 1 cup mixture into each of four 8-ounce serving glasses. Serve immediately, with thick straws or iced tea spoons; this mixture must be crushed and reblended if stored.

Makes 4 servings. Each serving has 96 calories.

Mock Egg Nog

2 cups crushed ice
1 cup water
¾ cup nonfat dry milk powder
2 teaspoons rum extract
1½ teaspoons vanilla extract
cinnamon

1. In electric blender, blend 1 cup of the crushed ice, the water, dry milk powder and rum and vanilla extracts at high speed until thick and smooth, about 30 to 45 seconds.

2. Add remaining crushed ice and blend at high speed 30 seconds longer.

3. Pour 1 cup mixture into each of four 8-ounce serving glasses. Serve immediately, sprinkling each with cinnamon.

Makes 4 servings. Each serving has 50 calories.

Mimosa

1 cup crushed ice
1 cup vanilla ice milk
1 cup fresh orange juice
one 10-ounce bottle low-calorie ginger ale

1. In electric blender, blend crushed ice, ice milk and orange juice at high speed for 5 seconds.

2. Pour ¾ cup mixture into each of four 8-ounce serving glasses, adding approximately ¼ cup ginger ale to each. Serve immediately, with two thick straws or iced tea spoon in each; this dessert cannot be stored.

Makes 4 servings. Each serving has 79 calories.

Pineapple-Banana Smooth

1 cup crushed ice
1 cup water
one 8-ounce can crushed pineapple in natural juices
1 medium banana, peeled and sliced
½ cup nonfat dry milk powder

1. In electric blender, blend all ingredients at high speed until thick and smooth, about 30 to 45 seconds.

2. Pour 1 cup mixture into each of four 8-ounce serving glasses. Serve immediately, with two thick straws or iced tea spoon in each; this dessert cannot be stored.

Makes 4 servings. Each serving has 88 calories.

Orange-Pineapple Slush

2 cups crushed ice

one 8-ounce can crushed pineapple in natural juices

1 cup orange juice

¼ cup water

¼ cup nonfat dry milk powder

1. In electric blender, blend 1 cup of the crushed ice, the undrained crushed pineapple, orange juice, water and dry milk powder at high speed until smooth, about 30 seconds.

2. Add remaining crushed ice and blend until thick and smooth, about 30 seconds longer.

3. Pour 1 cup mixture into each of four 8-ounce serving glasses. Serve immediately, with two thick straws or iced tea spoon in each.

Makes 4 servings. Each serving has 90 calories.

Strawberry Fizz

1 cup vanilla ice milk

one 16-ounce package frozen unsweetened strawberries, thawed

2 cups low-calorie ginger ale

1. In electric blender, blend ice milk and thawed strawberries at high speed until thick and smooth, about 10 seconds.

2. Pour ¾ cup mixture into each of four 12-ounce serving glasses, adding ½ cup ginger ale to each. Serve immediately, with two thick straws in each.

Makes 4 servings. Each serving has 75 calories.

Ambrosia Parfait

one 11-ounce can mandarin oranges, drained

one 8¾-ounce can apricot halves, drained

1⅓ cups vanilla ice milk

2 tablespoons shredded coconut

1. In electric blender, blend drained oranges and apricots at high speed for 5 seconds.

2. Spoon 1 teaspoon mixture into each of 4 small parfait glasses. Fill each glass with ⅓ cup ice milk; top each with one-fourth of remaining fruit mixture and sprinkle each with 1½ teaspoons coconut.

3. Serve immediately, or freeze for up to 30 minutes, then serve.

Makes 4 servings. Each serving has 162 calories.

Raisin Parfait

1 tablespoon diet margarine
½ teaspoon flour
1 cup water
¼ cup golden raisins
1 tablespoon granulated sugar replacement
¼ teaspoon grated lemon rind
dash of salt
1⅓ cups vanilla ice milk

1. Melt diet margarine in small saucepan over low heat; stir in flour. Slowly blend in water; bring to boiling point, stirring constantly. Add golden raisins, sugar replacement, lemon rind and salt. Simmer, covered, for 15 minutes; keep warm.

2. Spoon ⅓ cup vanilla ice milk into each of 4 parfait glasses; top with 1 tablespoon sauce. Serve immediately; chill surplus sauce for other desserts.

Makes 4 servings. Each serving has 101 calories.

Cantaloupe Ice

1 medium cantaloupe, cut into chunks
1 tablespoon lemon juice
1 teaspoon granulated sugar replacement
¼ teaspoon salt

1. In electric blender, blend 1 cup of the cantaloupe chunks, the lemon juice, sugar replacement and salt at high speed until smooth, about 30 seconds.

2. Add remaining cantaloupe chunks; blend at high speed until smooth, about 30 to 45 seconds. Pour into 8 x 8 x 2-inch metal pan; freeze until semi-firm, about 1 hour.

3. Place mixture in large bowl; using electric mixer at high speed, beat until smooth. Return to metal pan; freeze until firm, about 2 hours. To serve, spoon 1 cup mixture into each of 4 dessert glasses.

Makes 4 servings. Each serving has 19 calories.

Frozen Coffee Cream

1 envelope unflavored gelatin
¼ cup cold water
1 cup boiling water
1 cup lowfat unflavored yogurt
⅔ cup nonfat dry milk powder
3 tablespoons granulated
  sugar replacement
1½ teaspoons instant coffee

1. Sprinkle gelatin over cold water in blender container; let stand for 5 minutes to soften. Add boiling water and blend at medium speed until gelatin is dissolved.

2. Add yogurt, dry milk powder, sugar replacement and instant coffee. Blend mixture at high speed until smooth. Pour into 8 x 8 x 2-inch metal pan; freeze until semi-set, about 1 hour.

3. Place mixture in large bowl; using electric mixer at high speed, beat until smooth. Return to metal pan; freeze until firm, about 2 hours. To serve, spoon 1 cup mixture into each of 4 dessert dishes.

Makes 4 servings. Each serving has 85 calories.

Grape Slush

one 8-ounce can crushed
  pineapple in natural juices
2 cups grape juice
¼ cup orange juice
¼ cup granulated sugar
  replacement

1. In electric blender, blend all ingredients at high speed for 5 seconds. Pour mixture into 8 x 8 x 2-inch metal pan; freeze until firm, about 1 to 1½ hours.

2. To serve, let stand at room temperature for a few minutes to soften; then stir with metal spoon, breaking up mixture until slushy. Spoon ¾ cup mixture into each of 4 serving dishes.

Makes 4 servings. Each serving has 46 calories.

Frozen Peach Milk Dessert

1½ cups nonfat dry milk powder
¼ cup water
2 tablespoons lemon juice
2 tablespoons granulated sugar replacement
one 8-ounce can sliced peaches

1. Using electric mixer at high speed, beat dry milk powder, water, lemon juice and sugar replacement in large bowl until thick and smooth.

2. In electric blender, puree peach slices at high speed until smooth. Add to milk mixture; using electric mixer at high speed, beat until completely blended and fluffy. Pour mixture into 8 x 8 x 2-inch metal pan; freeze until firm, about 3 hours. To serve, spoon ½ cup peach mixture into each of 4 small parfait glasses.

Makes 4 servings. Each serving has 139 calories.

Raspberry Sherbet

1 envelope unflavored gelatin
¾ cup cold water
two 10-ounce packages frozen raspberries, thawed

1. Sprinkle gelatin over cold water in small saucepan; let stand for 5 minutes to soften. Place over low heat just until gelatin is dissolved.

2. In electric blender, blend raspberries at high speed until smooth, about 10 to 15 seconds. Add dissolved gelatin; blend 5 seconds longer.

3. Pour mixture into 8 x 8 x 2-inch metal pan; freeze until semi-set, about 1 hour. Place mixture in large bowl; using electric mixer at high speed, beat until smooth and fluffy.

4. Return mixture to pan; freeze until firm, about 2 hours. To serve, spoon ½ cup mixture into each of 4 dessert dishes.

Makes 4 servings. Each serving has 147 calories.

Frozen Raspberry Yogurt Cream

1 envelope unflavored gelatin
¼ cup cold water
1 cup boiling water
one 10-ounce package frozen
  raspberries, thawed
1 cup lowfat unflavored yogurt
⅔ cup nonfat dry milk powder
¼ teaspoon salt

1. Sprinkle gelatin over cold water in blender container; let stand for 5 minutes to soften. Add boiling water and blend at medium speed until gelatin is dissolved.

2. Add thawed raspberries, yogurt, dry milk powder and salt. Blend at high speed until smooth; pour into 8 x 8 x 2-inch metal pan and freeze until semi-set, about 1 hour.

3. Place mixture in large bowl; using electric mixer at high speed, beat until smooth. Return to metal pan; freeze until firm, about 2 hours. To serve, spoon 1 cup mixture into each of 4 dessert dishes.

Makes 4 servings. Each serving has 149 calories.

Frozen Strawberry Milk Dessert

1½ cups nonfat dry milk
  powder
¼ cup water
2 tablespoons lemon juice
2 tablespoons granulated
  sugar replacement
1 cup frozen unsweetened
  strawberries, thawed and
  crushed with juice

1. Using electric mixer at high speed, beat dry milk powder, water, lemon juice and sugar replacement in large bowl until smooth and thick. Add thawed, undrained strawberries; using mixer at high speed, beat until completely blended and fluffy.

2. Pour mixture into 8 x 8 x 2-inch metal pan, making sure fruit is evenly distributed. Freeze until firm, about 3 hours. To serve, spoon ½ cup mixture into each of 4 small parfait glasses.

Makes 4 servings. Each serving has 157 calories.

Calorie-Cut Classics

Here they are — the heavy artillery without the heavy calories. After those special dinners, dig into Baked Alaska, Cherries Jubilee, Strawberry Shortcake, Chocolate Mousse — 30 all-time classics you thought you'd never eat again.

How is it done? The Baked Alaska tops angel food cake with strawberry ice milk before it's cloaked in meringue. The Chocolate Mousse is made with evaporated skim milk instead of cream. Full of real milk chocolate, it comes in at 129 calories a serving.

And how about Mocha Eclairs filled with yogurt at 76 calories each, or a no-fuss Apricot Mousse whipped up to a frothy 69 calories a serving? These sweet savers certainly put dieting in a new light.

There's a recipe for every occasion: wholesome fruit dishes for the kids and sophisticated desserts for adults perfumed with wine and liqueurs; recipes for chocolate lovers and nut freaks; pies, parfaits and custards.

Some of these recipes do call for a sugar replacement. The amounts are small, however, and if you've decided to avoid saccharin, you can substitute one teaspoon of granulated sugar for each tablespoon of sugar replacement. (One teaspoon of sugar has 13 calories.)

Whatever the occasion — a birthday, anniversary or the day you reach your dieting goal — let it be a real celebration with one of these fabulous classic desserts.

Baked Alaska

1 quart strawberry ice milk
one 16-ounce package angel food cake mix
4 egg whites
½ teaspoon cream of tartar
⅓ cup granulated sugar replacement
½ teaspoon vanilla extract

1. Press strawberry ice milk into foil-lined 8 x 8 x 2-inch baking pan; freeze.

2. Preheat oven to 425° F or to temperature suggested on cake mix box. Prepare cake mix according to label directions. Divide batter between two 8 x 8 x 2-inch baking pans lined with waxed paper. Bake for 30 to 35 minutes, until cake tester inserted in center comes out clean. Remove cake from pans and place on wire rack to cool.

3. Place one cake layer on foil-lined cookie sheet; wrap and freeze second layer for dessert another day. Unmold strawberry ice milk onto cake and peel off foil; freeze.

4. Preheat oven to 500° F.

5. Using electric mixer at high speed, beat egg whites and cream of tartar in medium bowl until frothy. Beat in sugar replacement, 1 tablespoon at a time, and vanilla extract until egg whites are stiff.

6. Using small metal spatula, frost cake and ice milk layers with meringue to cover completely. Bake for 3 to 5 minutes or until meringue is lightly browned. Serve immediately.

Makes 16 servings. Each serving has 112 calories.

Note: Cut as many servings as desired from Baked Alaska and immediately put remainder in freezer.

◯ *CalorieSaving Tip:* Read the labels on all the ice milk containers in the store, and make your Baked Alaska (above) with the kind that has the lowest calorie count. You can store your surplus Baked Alaska in the freezer by placing toothpicks in the meringue and covering the dessert completely with plastic wrap; the toothpicks keep the plastic from touching the meringue. Baked Alaska will keep for a week, though the meringue will toughen slightly.

Cinnamon Baked Apples

4 apples, 2½ inches in
  diameter
2 tablespoons brown sugar
2 tablespoons granulated
  sugar replacement
1 tablespoon diet margarine
¼ teaspoon cinnamon
boiling water

1. Preheat oven to 375° F.

2. Wash and dry apples; pierce skins with fork. Remove core of each to within ½ inch of bottom. Place apples in baking dish.

3. In small bowl, combine brown sugar, sugar replacement, diet margarine and cinnamon. Fill center of each apple with one-fourth of sugar mixture. Pour boiling water into baking pan to depth of ¼ inch.

4. Bake for 30 minutes or until apples are fork-tender, basting with pan juices several times during cooking. Serve hot or cold.

Makes 4 servings. Each serving has 119 calories.

Apple Brown Betty

2 tablespoons diet margarine
2 slices day-old white bread,
  cubed
½ teaspoon cinnamon
4 medium apples
½ cup granulated sugar
  replacement
½ teaspoon allspice
2 tablespoons lemon juice

1. Melt diet margarine in medium skillet over medium heat; add bread cubes and sauté until brown, stirring occasionally. Remove from heat; sprinkle with cinnamon.

2. Preheat oven to 350° F.

3. Peel, core and slice apples; place in medium bowl. Toss with sugar replacement, allspice and lemon juice. Place in lightly greased 8 x 8 x 2-inch baking dish. Cover dish with foil. Bake for 35 to 40 minutes or until apples are tender.

Makes 6 servings. Each serving has 94 calories.

Honeyed Apple Pie

one 10-ounce package
  piecrust mix
5 cups sliced apples
½ cup honey
2 teaspoons lemon juice
¼ teaspoon cinnamon
¼ teaspoon nutmeg
dash of salt
2 tablespoons diet margarine

1. Preheat oven to 425° F.

2. Prepare piecrust mix according to label directions; form dough into ball, wrap and chill.

3. In large bowl, gently stir together apple slices, honey, lemon juice, cinnamon, nutmeg and salt. Set aside.

4. Divide piecrust dough into thirds; roll out two thirds to line 8-inch pie plate. Roll out remaining third to form top crust.

5. Arrange apple mixture in pie shell; dot with diet margarine. Set top crust in position; seal and crimp edges. Make slits in top crust to allow steam to escape.

6. Bake for 40 to 50 minutes, until pastry is golden brown and apples are tender. Cool for 10 minutes before cutting.

Makes 10 servings. Each serving has 240 calories.

Apricot Mousse

one 17-ounce can apricot
  halves in light syrup
1 envelope unflavored gelatin
1 tablespoon lemon juice
1 teaspoon grated lemon rind
¼ cup ice water

1. Drain ¼ cup of the apricot syrup into small saucepan. Sprinkle gelatin over syrup; let stand for 5 minutes to soften. Place over low heat just until gelatin is dissolved, stirring constantly.

2. In electric blender, puree apricot halves and remaining syrup at high speed until smooth, about 10 seconds.

3. In medium bowl, combine gelatin mixture, pureed apricots and ice water; stir to blend well. Chill mixture until almost set, about 1 hour.

4. Using electric mixer at high speed, beat mixture until frothy. Spoon into 4 individual dessert dishes.

Makes 4 servings. Each serving has 69 calories.

Baked Bananas with Almonds and Honey

4 small bananas
2 tablespoons lemon juice
2 tablespoons honey
½ cup unsweetened applesauce
2 tablespoons chopped toasted almonds

1. Preheat oven to 375° F.

2. Peel bananas and slice lengthwise. Place in lightly greased 9 x 9 x 2-inch baking dish; sprinkle with lemon juice and drizzle 1½ teaspoons honey over each banana.

3. Cover dish with foil; bake for 25 to 30 minutes. Serve hot, topping each serving with 2 tablespoons applesauce and 1½ teaspoons toasted almonds.

Makes 4 servings. Each serving has 133 calories.

Favorite Banana Parfait

1 tablespoon diet margarine
1 medium banana, sliced
2 tablespoons honey
2 tablespoons orange juice
2 tablespoons chopped walnuts
1 tablespoon rum
1 pint vanilla ice milk

1. Melt diet margarine in medium skillet over medium heat; add banana slices and cook, stirring constantly, until soft.

2. Add honey; cook until banana is completely soft. Stir in orange juice and chopped walnuts. Pour rum over mixture and keep warm.

3. To serve, place ½ cup vanilla ice milk in each of 4 individual dessert glasses. Ignite banana sauce and divide among servings of ice milk.

Makes 4 servings. Each serving has 94 calories.

◎ *CalorieSaving Tip:* Remember that rum is highly caloric; rum extract is a low-calorie substitute. Since all alcohol is sugar based, it's a dietary extravagance—try not to use it (except for special occasions). The liquors that are loaded with the most calories are high-proof, very sweet and fruit based.

Foamy Blancmange

1 envelope unflavored gelatin
¼ cup cold water
2 cups skim milk
2 tablespoons granulated sugar replacement
¼ teaspoon salt
1 teaspoon vanilla extract

1. Sprinkle gelatin over cold water in medium bowl; let stand for 5 minutes to soften.

2. In medium saucepan, combine skim milk, sugar replacement and salt. Heat to boiling point over medium heat. Pour boiling liquid over gelatin mixture; stir to dissolve gelatin completely. Add vanilla extract. Chill for at least 1½ hours or until almost set.

3. Using electric mixer at high speed, beat blancmange until very frothy. Spoon into four 10-ounce custard cups.

Makes 4 servings. Each serving has 62 calories.

Cheese Blintzes

2 eggs
3 tablespoons flour
¼ cup skim milk
2 tablespoons diet margarine
1 cup lowfat, small curd cottage cheese
1 teaspoon vanilla extract
½ teaspoon grated lemon rind
1 tablespoon sugar
½ teaspoon cinnamon

1. In medium bowl, beat together eggs, flour, skim milk and 1 tablespoon of the diet margarine until smooth. Let batter stand for 20 minutes.

2. Place 5-inch omelet pan with nonstick finish over medium heat; heat for 2 minutes. Pour in enough batter to cover bottom of pan with thin coating, about 2 to 3 tablespoons. Cook crêpe on one side only until pale gold. Place cooked side down on clean dish towel. Repeat until all batter is used to make 6 crêpes.

3. Press cottage cheese through sieve into medium bowl. Add vanilla extract and lemon rind; beat until smooth. Divide mixture among crêpes, setting filling at one edge of each crêpe. Roll up jelly-roll fashion, turning sides to contain filling.

4. Melt remaining diet margarine in large skillet over medium heat. Place blintzes seam side down in skillet and cook until light brown, turning once. Sprinkle with sugar and cinnamon; serve immediately.

Makes 4 servings. Each serving of 1½ blintzes has 141 calories.

Ice Bombe

1 pint vanilla ice milk
1 pint strawberry ice milk
1 pint chocolate ice milk

1. Chill 1-quart mold in freezer. Soften vanilla ice milk slightly; pack tightly into mold. Freeze until firm, about 1 hour.

2. Soften strawberry ice milk slightly; pack on top of vanilla ice milk. Freeze for 1 hour.

3. Repeat with chocolate ice milk. Freeze for 6 hours. Dip mold into cool water, then unmold bombe onto chilled platter. Freeze until serving time.

Makes 8 servings. Each serving has 150 calories.

Note: Return surplus to freezer if not served immediately.

Spicy Bread Pudding

3 slices day-old white bread, cut into ⅓-inch cubes
1¼ cups skim milk
2 egg yolks
2 tablespoons sugar
½ teaspoon cinnamon
½ teaspoon vanilla extract
⅛ teaspoon salt

1. Preheat oven to 350° F.

2. Place bread cubes in lightly greased 1-quart baking dish.

3. Warm skim milk in medium saucepan over low heat. Using fork or wire whisk, beat together egg yolks, sugar, cinnamon, vanilla extract and salt in small bowl. Beat in warm milk.

4. Pour egg-milk mixture over bread cubes. Bake for 50 to 55 minutes, until slightly puffed and crisp on top and bubbling around edges. Cool slightly before serving.

Makes 4 servings. Each serving has 154 calories.

Ⓞ *CalorieSaving Tip:* If a recipe calls for greasing your cooking container, use the smallest amount of diet margarine possible to prevent sticking. Better yet, use baking dishes, pans and sheets with a nonstick finish or give your pans a light dusting from a can of vegetable spray.

Butterscotch Pudding

2 tablepoons brown sugar
2 tablespoons cornstarch
⅛ teaspoon salt
2 cups skim milk
2 egg yolks
1 teaspoon vanilla extract

1. In medium saucepan, blend together brown sugar, cornstarch and salt.

2. In medium bowl, beat together milk and egg yolks with wire whisk. Gradually add to sugar mixture, whisking to keep smooth.

3. Bring mixture to boiling point over medium heat, stirring constantly to keep smooth. Remove from heat; stir in vanilla extract.

4. Stir to cool slightly. Divide mixture among 4 dessert dishes; chill until serving time.

Makes 4 servings. Each serving has 123 calories.

Coffee Charlotte Russe

4 slices store-bought pound cake, ¼ inch thick
½ envelope unflavored gelatin
2 tablespoons water
¼ cup skim milk
1 teaspoon instant freeze-dried coffee
½ cup heavy cream
2 tablespoons granulated sugar replacement

1. Cut each slice of pound cake into thin strips. Use to line sides of 4 small dessert glasses. Set aside.

2. Sprinkle gelatin over water in small bowl; let stand for 5 minutes to soften.

3. Bring milk to boiling point in small saucepan over low heat; pour over gelatin. Add instant coffee; stir to dissolve. Cool.

4. Using electric mixer at high speed, beat cream in medium bowl until soft peaks form. Add sugar replacement and beat until stiff.

5. Fold whipped cream into gelatin mixture; divide mixture among dessert glasses. Chill until firm, about 1 hour.

Makes 4 servings. Each serving has 129 calories.

Slim Pineapple Cheesecake

⅔ cup graham cracker crumbs

2 tablespoons diet margarine, melted

one 16-ounce container lowfat cottage cheese

1 cup evaporated skim milk

⅓ cup granulated sugar replacement

2 tablespoons flour

4 eggs

1 tablespoon lemon juice

1 teaspoon vanilla extract

½ teaspoon cinnamon

one 8-ounce can crushed pineapple in natural juices, drained

1. Preheat oven to 325° F.

2. In small bowl, combine graham cracker crumbs and melted diet margarine with fork. Pat over bottom of 9-inch springform pan; set aside.

3. Press cottage cheese through sieve into large bowl. Add evaporated milk, ¼ cup of the sugar replacement, the flour, eggs, lemon juice and vanilla extract. Using electric mixer at high speed, beat mixture until smooth.

4. Pour filling into piecrust in springform pan; bake for 1 hour. Turn off heat; leave cheesecake in oven 1 hour longer. Remove from oven; sprinkle surface with remaining sugar replacement mixed with cinnamon. Cool completely. Top with drained pineapple.

Makes 10 servings. Each serving has 128 calories. Shown on front cover.

Cherries Jubilee

1 cup black cherry preserves

1 teaspoon grated lemon rind

2 tablespoons brandy

1⅓ cups vanilla ice milk

1. In small chafing dish, fondue pot or saucepan, blend preserves and lemon rind; cook over low heat until mixture bubbles. Add brandy and ignite. Keep warm.

2. Spoon ⅓ cup vanilla ice milk into each of 4 dessert dishes; top each with 2 tablespoons sauce. Serve immediately. Chill surplus sauce for later use.

Makes 4 servings. Each serving has 136 calories. Shown on page 72.

Chocolate Mousse

4 ounces milk chocolate
½ cup evaporated skim milk
2 tablespoons granulated sugar replacement
2 eggs, separated
½ teaspoon vanilla extract

1. Heat chocolate, evaporated milk and sugar replacement in medium saucepan over very low heat, stirring constantly until chocolate is melted. Remove from heat.

2. Beat egg yolks in small bowl. Pour a little chocolate mixture over eggs and stir until thoroughly blended. Pour egg yolk mixture into saucepan; add vanilla extract. Heat until mixture thickens slightly, stirring constantly. Remove from heat; pour into large bowl; cool slightly.

3. Using electric mixer at high speed, beat egg whites in medium bowl until soft peaks form. Using rubber spatula, gently fold egg whites into chocolate mixture. Divide mixture among six 6-ounce custard cups or individual soufflé dishes.

Makes 6 servings. Each serving has 129 calories.

Dame Blanche

one 16-ounce can peach halves
½ cup canned crushed pineapple in natural juices
4 maraschino cherries, quartered
1⅓ cups vanilla ice milk

1. Drain peach halves thoroughly; place hollow side up in 4 individual dessert dishes. Set aside.

2. In electric blender, blend crushed pineapple and maraschino cherries at high speed for 5 seconds.

3. Spoon ⅓ cup ice milk on top of each dish of peach halves; spoon one-fourth of pineapple mixture over each.

Makes 4 servings. Each serving has 153 calories.

Mocha Eclairs

¼ cup diet margarine
½ cup water
½ cup all-purpose flour
3 eggs
one 16-ounce container lowfat
   unflavored yogurt
2 tablespoons granulated
   sugar replacement
2 teaspoons instant coffee
2 teaspoons cocoa powder

1. Preheat oven to 375° F.

2. Combine diet margarine and water in medium saucepan over medium heat; stir constantly until margarine melts and water boils.

3. Add flour all at once; beat until mixture leaves side of pan and forms a smooth ball. Remove from heat. Using electric mixer at medium speed, beat in eggs, one at a time, until mixture is smooth.

4. Form dough into 3 x 1-inch oblongs on cookie sheet with nonstick finish. Bake for 30 minutes or until lightly browned. Remove to wire rack to cool.

5. In medium bowl, blend yogurt, sugar replacement, instant coffee and cocoa powder. Fill eclairs by slitting open tops and spooning in mocha yogurt mixture.

Makes 12 servings. Each serving has 76 calories.

Sugar-Broiled Grapefruit

2 yellow grapefruit, 4 inches in
   diameter
¼ cup orange juice
¼ cup brown sugar, firmly
   packed
1 teaspoon grated orange rind
4 maraschino cherries

1. Preheat broiler.

2. Cut grapefruit in half; remove seeds. Using sharp knife, cut around edges and sections to free flesh. Remove tough fibrous center. Place grapefruit in shallow baking dish.

3. Sprinkle each grapefruit half with 1 tablespoon orange juice and one-fourth of mixture of brown sugar and grated orange rind. Place cherry in center of each. Broil grapefruit 6 inches from heat for 8 to 10 minutes or until lightly browned.

Makes 4 servings. Each serving has 100 calories.

Lemon Chiffon Pie

one 8-inch Zwieback Piecrust
  (recipe below)

FILLING

1   envelope unflavored gelatin
¼   cup cold water
4   eggs, separated
½   cup honey
½   cup lemon juice
1   teaspoon grated lemon rind

1. Prepare Zwieback Piecrust.

2. Meanwhile, prepare pie filling by sprinkling gelatin over cold water in small bowl; let stand for 5 minutes to soften.

3. Using electric mixer at medium speed, beat egg yolks in top of double boiler until lemon colored. Add honey, lemon juice and lemon rind.

4. Cook over simmering water until thickened, stirring constantly. Stir in softened gelatin to dissolve; cool. Using electric mixer at high speed, beat egg whites in large bowl until stiff. Fold into lemon mixture.

5. Spoon mixture into baked Zwieback Piecrust. Chill for at least 2 hours.

Makes 12 servings. Each serving has 112 calories.

Zwieback Piecrust

8   zwieback, finely crushed
¼   cup nonfat dry milk powder
1   tablespoon confectioners'
    sugar
1   tablespoon diet margarine,
    melted
1   tablespoon skim milk

1. Preheat oven to 375° F.

2. In medium bowl, combine zwieback crumbs, dry milk powder and confectioners' sugar. Using fork, stir in melted diet margarine and skim milk.

3. Press mixture over bottom and sides of 8-inch pie plate. Bake for 8 to 10 minutes. Cool completely on wire rack.

Makes one 8-inch pie shell.

◎ *CalorieSaving Tip:* Use confectioners' sugar rather than granulated sugar to flavor piecrust. While confectioners' has no fewer calories than granulated, you can use less of it because it spreads more evenly throughout the crust mixture.

Lemon Mousse

1 cup evaporated skim milk
¼ cup lemon juice
¼ cup sugar
1 teaspoon grated lemon rind
2 eggs, separated

1. Heat evaporated milk, lemon juice, sugar and lemon rind in top of double boiler over boiling water. Cook, stirring constantly, until sugar is dissolved.

2. In small bowl, beat egg yolks with fork; beat in a little hot lemon mixture, then pour egg yolks into pan. Cook, stirring constantly, until mixture thickens and lightly coats back of wooden spoon. Remove from heat; cool, then chill.

3. Using electric mixer at high speed, beat egg whites in medium bowl until stiff peaks form. Fold chilled lemon mixture into egg whites. Spoon into four 6-ounce custard cups or individual soufflé dishes; chill.

Makes 4 servings. Each serving has 100 calories.

Peach Melba

2 fresh peaches, 2 inches in diameter, or 2 canned peach halves
half of 10-ounce package frozen raspberries, thawed and drained
1 pint vanilla ice milk

1. Peel fresh peaches and cut into thin slices; or drain canned peach halves and slice. Combine with raspberries in medium bowl; chill.

2. Place ½ cup vanilla ice milk in each of 4 dessert glasses. Freeze.

3. To serve, divide peach mixture among dessert glasses to top ice milk.

Makes 4 servings. Each serving has 153 calories.

Cream-Filled Peaches

one 16-ounce can peach
 halves
½ cup heavy cream
1 tablespoon granulated sugar
 replacement
¼ teaspoon cinnamon

1. Drain peaches thoroughly. Place 2 peach halves cut side up in 4 individual dessert dishes; chill.

2. Using electric mixer at high speed, beat cream in medium bowl until soft peaks form. Sprinkle with sugar replacement; beat cream until stiff. Sprinkle with cinnamon while beating slowly. Top each peach serving with one-fourth of whipped cream mixture.

Makes 4 servings. Each serving has 174 calories.

Pears Hélène

2 ripe pears
1 tablespoon lemon juice
¼ cup honey
½ cup evaporated skim milk
⅓ cup carob powder or
 cocoa powder
1 teaspoon diet margarine
¼ teaspoon vanilla extract
1 pint vanilla ice milk

1. Pare pears and cut lengthwise in half; using small teaspoon, remove core. Place pears in large skillet with ½ inch water.

2. Add lemon juice and 1 tablespoon of the honey. Simmer, covered, over low heat until pears are tender. Drain and place cut side up in 4 individual serving dishes. Cool and chill.

3. Meanwhile, blend milk and carob or cocoa powder in small saucepan. Heat to boiling point, stirring constantly. Remove from heat; stir in remaining 3 tablespoons honey, the diet margarine and vanilla extract.

4. Place ¼-cup scoop ice milk on top of each pear half and spoon 2 tablespoons sauce over each. Serve immediately.

Makes 4 servings. Each serving has 227 calories.

Poached Pears in White Wine

¾ cup water
4 medium pears, pared and sliced
1 cup dry white wine
2 tablespoons granulated sugar replacement
1½ teaspoons grated lemon rind

1. Bring water to boiling point in large skillet over medium heat; add pears. Reduce heat to low and simmer, covered, for 10 to 15 minutes or until fork-tender.

2. Stir in white wine, sugar replacement and lemon rind. Pour into serving bowl; chill.

Makes 4 servings. Each serving has 66 calories.

Pumpkin Pie

one 10-ounce package piecrust mix
1¼ cups evaporated skim milk
2 eggs
1 cup canned pumpkin
½ cup granulated sugar replacement
2 teaspoons pumpkin pie spice
¼ teaspoon ginger

1. Preheat oven to 425° F.

2. Prepare piecrust according to label directions. Divide in half; wrap and refrigerate one portion for another use. Roll out remaining half to line 8-inch pie plate. Trim and flute edge of pastry.

3. Using electric mixer at medium speed, beat remaining ingredients in large bowl until smooth.

4. Pour mixture into pie shell; bake for 10 minutes. Reduce oven heat to 350° F; bake 40 to 50 minutes longer or until knife inserted in center comes out clean. Cool completely.

Makes 10 servings. Each serving has 105 calories.

◎ *CalorieSaving Tip:* Don't roll out pastry on a flour-dusted board—the flour insidiously adds calories to your dessert. Instead, place the dough between two sheets of waxed paper or plastic wrap and roll it out to the size you require. Peel off the top paper and flip the pastry over into the pie plate. Peel off the second paper layer and gently ease the pastry into the pan, then flute the edge.

Creamy Rice Pudding

⅓ cup uncooked long-grain rice
¼ cup water
2 cups skim milk
2 tablespoons sugar
⅛ teaspoon salt
1 egg
1 teaspoon vanilla extract
¼ cup golden raisins

1. In large saucepan, combine rice, water, 1½ cups of the skim milk, the sugar and salt. Bring to boiling point over medium heat, stirring constantly.

2. Reduce heat to low and simmer, covered, until rice is tender and mixture thickens and bubbles slowly and evenly, about 15 to 20 minutes.

3. Meanwhile, use wire whisk to beat together remaining skim milk, the egg and vanilla extract in small bowl. Add to cooked rice mixture along with golden raisins.

4. Cook until thick and creamy, about 3 to 4 minutes, stirring constantly. Divide among 4 dessert dishes; chill.

Makes 4 servings. Each serving has 136 calories.

Rice Pudding Supreme

⅓ cup uncooked long-grain rice
⅔ cup water
3 eggs, separated
½ cup sugar
3 cups skim milk
1 teaspoon vanilla extract
¼ teaspoon nutmeg

1. In small saucepan, blend rice and water; cook, covered, over low heat until rice is tender, about 20 minutes.

2. Meanwhile, blend egg yolks, ¼ cup of the sugar and the skim milk in medium saucepan. Cook over low heat, stirring constantly, until mixture lightly coats back of wooden spoon. Stir in cooked rice and vanilla extract. Pour into 1½-quart casserole, preferably with nonstick finish.

3. Preheat oven to 325° F.

4. Using electric mixer at high speed, beat egg whites in medium bowl until soft peaks form; gradually add remaining ¼ cup sugar, beating until egg whites are stiff. Swirl egg whites on top of rice mixture; sprinkle with nutmeg. Bake for 30 minutes. Serve hot or cold.

Makes 8 servings. Each serving has 124 calories.

Strawberry Shortcake

2 cups packaged biscuit mix

1 pound fresh strawberries, or one 16-ounce package frozen unsweetened strawberries, thawed

¼ cup unsweetened grapefruit juice

2 tablespoons granulated sugar replacement

¾ cup dry skim milk powder

¼ cup ice water

2 tablespoons diet margarine

1. Prepare biscuit mix according to label directions; cut dough into biscuits ½ inch thick and 2½ inches in diameter. Bake according to label directions. Reserve 2 biscuits for dessert. Cool, wrap and freeze remaining biscuits for later use.

2. Slice strawberries to measure 2 cups; toss with grapefruit juice and sugar replacement.

3. Using electric mixer at high speed, make "cream" by beating together skim milk powder and ice water in small bowl until frothy and stiff.

4. To assemble shortcake, split 2 biscuits in half and set halves on 4 individual dessert plates. Spread each with 1½ teaspoons diet margarine; top each with ½ cup sliced strawberries and juices and ¼ cup "cream."

Makes 4 servings. Each serving has 81 calories. Shown on page 71.

Zabaglione

4 eggs, separated

¼ cup confectioners' sugar

¼ cup Marsala wine

1. Using electric mixer at high speed, beat egg yolks and sugar in top of double boiler until light in color.

2. Set top of double boiler over boiling water over medium heat; continue to beat until mixture is foamy.

3. Slowly beat in Marsala wine; beat until mixture thickens and is doubled in volume. Remove from heat.

4. Using electric mixer at high speed, beat egg whites in medium bowl until stiff peaks form. Using rubber spatula, fold into yolk-wine mixture. Divide zabaglione among four 6-ounce parfait glasses.

Makes 4 servings. Each serving has 122 calories.

Index

DESSERTS FOR DIETERS